Erick Meyenberg:

Even When Fall Is Here

Text by Ruth Estévez

haudenschildGarage | DoppelHouse Press

To Chris Shea / A Chris Shea

This book is a fictionalized narrative of the meetings over the years 2015 to 2017 between the artist Erick Meyenberg, the landscape designer Chris Shea (1953–2018), and Eloisa Haudenschild conducted as part of the project *Even When Fall Is Here*, realized at the *haudenschild*Garage. Commissioned and organized by Haudenschild, the work takes as its site the garden of Haudenschild's home in the La Jolla area of San Diego, California.

The project's point of departure is a logbook by Shea, who worked with Haudenschild for many years. After he was diagnosed with a terminal illness in 2014, Shea dedicated himself to creating an instruction manual that would help Haudenschild keep her garden alive in the years to come. In the book, he matches photographs of the garden's plants with their corresponding species names, growth cycles, and color ranges. The images, taken over the course of two years, illustrate the passing of time and are a meaningful record of Shea's final months.

Meyenberg translated Shea's photographs into a suite of forty-five gouache-on-paper paintings, creating an abstract version of the journal by assigning, in a precise and almost obsessive fashion, a distinct series of colors to each plant in the garden. Meyenberg's composition includes blank fragments, silences that correspond to the physical and temporal flow of the garden itself.

These paintings serve as a preamble for a six-channel video installation in which Meyenberg accompanies Shea on a walk through the garden as the gardener explains his profound relationship with the plants. In a way, the multichannel video is a performed painting that describes the history of a living space through an objective observation of color. The video was displayed in Haudenschild's garden for just one day, blending with the actual landscape.

Although nothing described here is completely true, this text functions as a pentagram for inserting some of the notes, dialogues, and expressions written, recorded, or simply recalled for the achievement of this project. Despite the visual richness and multiple layers that constitute Meyenberg's work for the *haudenschild*Garage, it is the relationships and personal conversations among the protagonists that weave the fabric of this narrative, which includes phrases from subjective sources such as Meyenberg's memories, more precise notes—from personal emails to quotations from books on the different aspects of the history and genealogies of gardens—and texts reflecting on the use of language. This intertextual exercise integrates the story's two protagonists (Meyenberg and Shea), the project's mentor (Haudenschild), and the writer of this text (Estévez) as one multifaceted character.

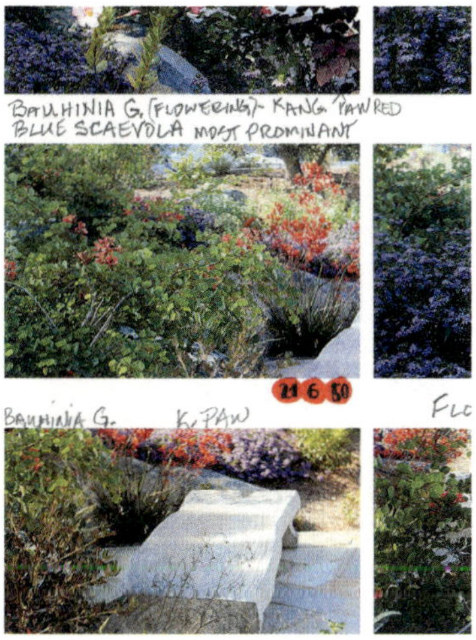

In all honesty, it was the garden that truly shaped his biography. For many, this small patch of land will disappear with time, as anecdotes always do (and perhaps it might only survive as a ruin). Public life, novel-writing, poems, and praises that accompanied him across the years ran perpendicularly to this green space. **"Light green, dark green,"** C would say, to define it in a few words.[1]

It never ceases to be paradoxical to have a CV devoted to language and at the same time to avoid writing—or rather, to stop feeling responsible for the use made of it. In any case, C was committed to a life devoted to the written narrative which he was able to pause in order to dedicate himself to other sorts of physical gestures. Today, I don't think these two things are incompatible.[2] It is from these gestures that these stories emerge, where work and a good dose of idleness blend. In this garden, C's essential work consisted of getting distracted, thinking of other things, fantasizing, taking his time to go to bed.

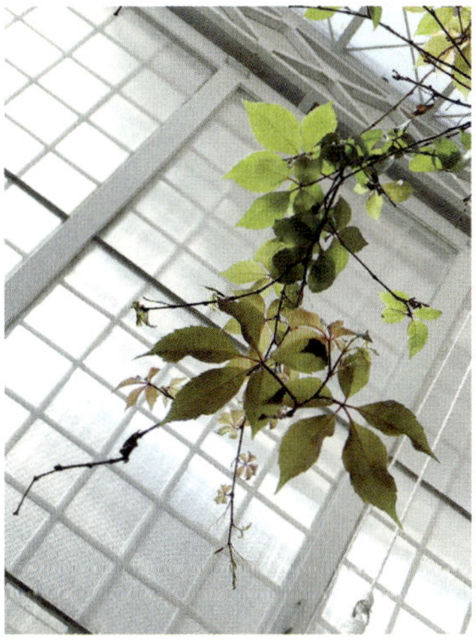

"I like gardening," said C. **"It's a place where I find myself when I need to lose myself."**[3]

From the outside, there was no room for misunderstanding, especially because C's garden was a private place—if not a *Secret Garden*—where guests rarely entered.[4] At the end of the side ground, he had a mount of some pretty height, leaving the wall of the enclosure breast-high, to look abroad into the fields.[5] In fact, if one walked several hundred meters away from that retaining wall, the entire panorama would be seen with faint clarity, an exercise which, regularly practiced, revealed color systems that expanded and changed over time: the garden was a meadow consisting of sinewy beds of perennials and grasses, planted by the thousands in intermingled groupings. [...] The combinations first come to life inside the house [of C], where colored pens scratch their way onto drafting paper in enigmatic hieroglyphics that read as art themselves.[6] (Or at least that is how I interpreted them.)

C liked saying his garden was a lateral garden.[7] It did not adjoin any central space beyond the open field itself, which was flanked by other lots, parcels, and cultivated areas. However, this laterality helped him continue expanding and "digging

1 Chris Shea, in conversation with Erick Meyenberg, 2015–17.

2 Fernando Sorrentino, *Siete conversaciones con Jorge Luis Borges* (Buenos Aires: Casa Pardo, 1974).

3 Shea, in conversation with Meyenberg.

4 Frances Hodgson Burnett's *The Secret Garden* (1911) is a classic of English children's literature.

5 Francis Bacon, "Of Gardens," in *Essays, Civil and Moral*. The Harvard Classics, vol. 3, part 1 (New York, P.F. Collier & Son, 1909–14), 181.

6 Adrian Higgins, "A new film takes us inside the mind—and the garden—of Piet Oudolf," *The Washington Post*, March 20, 2018. Web.

7 Bacon, 181.

holes somewhere else."[8] C modified the hierarchies of the garden. He amused himself by using as a guide practices considered secondary in regards to creation itself—such as the comment, annotation, gloss, or citation in regards to writing.[9] In reality, the garden was filled with many additional spaces that would never materialize. This practice of detour was a simple way to describe a more or less intuitive work, where the technique took shape through the semiotics of the calendar.

Thinking back, I don't believe C would have accepted my use of the garden, his or anyone else's, as a metaphor for anything. Nevertheless, now that it is my turn to speak of them—the garden and C—I cannot find a better strategy. **We are very accustomed to using the garden and the cycle of plants through the dialectic of comparison and plays on words, and it is complicated to get rid of them.**[10] C would not employ metaphors, hyperbaton, or anything exaggerating, converting into, or transitioning toward when speaking about his garden. The stories of the sides, like the plants that grew in his garden, aimed at nothing more than themselves: the unselfishness of natural colors.[11]

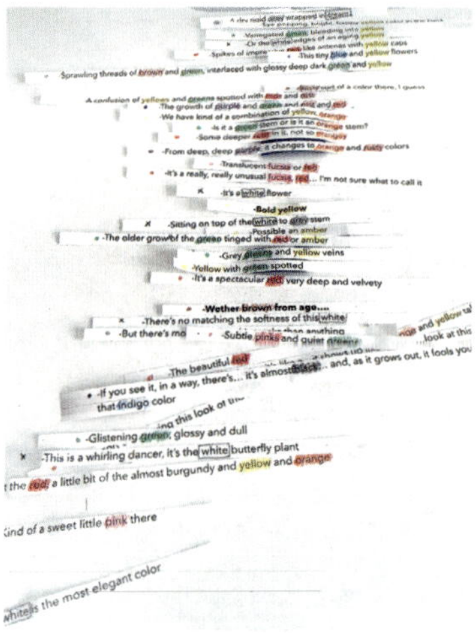

After we walked together through the garden for a couple of hours, C told me about a 1979 movie that tells the story of Chance, a gardener whose only experience of life consisted of cultivating a garden.[12] I don't imagine C was talking about himself, but I never really knew what came out of his memory and what was invented, or if his stories were the fruit of both. It could be that he was inviting me to reflect on the tricks that language plays compared to the honesty of his little piece of land. After an accident, Chance loses consciousness and is cared for by a wealthy couple who calls him Chauncey Gardiner after his name is misheard. The gardener becomes Gardiner, no longer Chance but Chauncey: Chauncey Gardiner. From simple to sophisticated, from random to precise, all because of a perverse play on words. "Don't you see?" said C. **"You don't have to use the garden as a metaphor for anything to avoid misunderstandings, even when these play to your advantage."**[13]

"Well, **I don't really have a real good name for that green,**" I told him, to protect

8 Edward de Bono, *Lateral Thinking; Creativity Step by Step* (New York: Harper & Row, 1970), 46.

9 Liliana Weinberg, "Jorge Luis Borges: lectura y escritura," *Revista de Estudios Latinoamericanos* 64 (2017): 71–98.

10 Shea, in conversation with Meyenberg.

11 Ibid.

12 *Being There* (1979), a film directed by Hal Ashby and based on the 1970 novel by Jerzy Kosiński.

13 Shea, in conversation with Meyenberg.

myself from his continuous evasions. **"It's somewhere between a grey-green and almost a blue-green,** don't you think?"[14] When I saw that he was not answering, I took a deep breath and dared to continue, **"There isn't a better way to express a feeling than through a garden—"**[15] "You're wrong," C interrupted. **"There is no fuller expression of vulgarity than a vulgar garden,"** he finished, contradicting me.[16] "When we speak of gardens, or rather, when we attempt to write about them," **he continued, calmly,** "our language is full of rhetoric, and this is related, perhaps, to an old literary antecedent."[17] **"Paradise?"** I asked. **"Perfection," he said. "Or at least the intention to make a green version of a place for rest and eternal relaxation; a place for flabby muscles."**

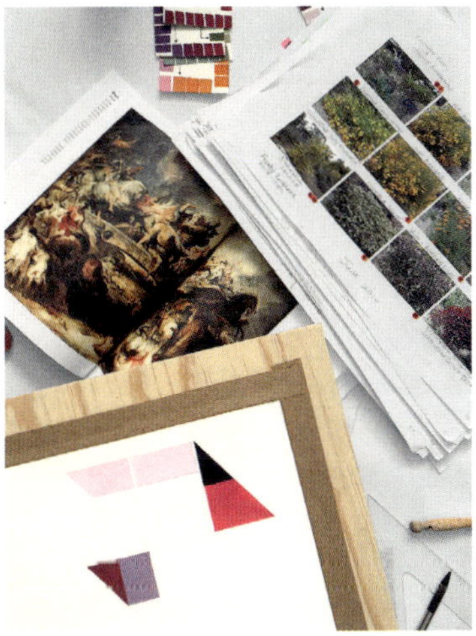

> [The Garden] is the greatest refreshment to the spirits of man; without which buildings and palaces are but gross handyworks: and a man shall ever see that when ages grow to civility and elegancy, men come to build stately, sooner than to garden finely; as if gardening were the greater perfection.[18]

"However," **C continued, after recalling Bacon,** "any gardener, from the simple window-ledger to the committed root-and-baller, will tell you that gardening is not actually about attaining perfection."[19] **Gardening as a creative project cannot be completed because it is an art that suffers from a deficit of organic survival. I imagine that communicating the aesthetic meaning of a garden to those who are not present demands, first of all, the use of language—which is, without a doubt, the least organic medium and doesn't provide many clues regarding that which was.** "**We can directly substitute words for a color palette,"** C told me, showing me an instruction manual he had assembled over two years. The notebook displayed all kinds of chromatic spectrums that revealed the different seasons of the garden through the changes of the plants. C had not forgotten to write the names of each of them, but he was careful not to use adjectives lightly.

"It is odd," he told me, **"how quickly the names of colors turn into adjectives that improve the noun that defines a flower. I like using colors as nouns, taking advantage of their limited gender inflection."**[20]

14 Shea, in conversation with Meyenberg.

15 Architect Luis Barragán's Pritzker Prize Laureate acceptance speech, delivered June 3, 1980. pritzkerprize.com.

16 Timothy Young, "A Garden Is Not a Metaphor," *JHI Blog*, *Journal of the History of Ideas*, March 19, 2018. jhiblog.org.

17 Bacon, 211.

18 Young.

19 Ibid.

20 Shea, in conversation with Meyenberg.

Hello Eloisa,

The following is a list of the majority of the trees in the garden. There are a few trees and large bushes not yet included. The trees below are listed in no particular order.

I thought the trees would be a good place to start. I have listed first the botanical name followed by the common name or names, the country of origin and its designation as either evergreen, semi-evergreen, or deciduous.

This seems to be a good way to stimulate discussion about the need to use "native" trees and plants vs. "immigrants". As you will see, few of our actual specimen trees or plants are native to or originating in our area. Though most are "immigrants," they have become pretty comfortable here and have, for the most part, been part of the southern California landscape for as long or longer than I have been in the business... many have been here for generations, if not since the beginning of the colonization of California.

Definitely, "native" plants are those that existed in California prior to the arrival of Europeans and colonists in the latter years of the 1700s. In my world, small though it may be, I have come to consider "native" to be those plants and trees that I have lived with, known about, worked with, and enjoyed for my last 40 years of business and life. In this garden that you and I have together created, so many of our most desirable and dependable landscape anchors would be considered non-native to experts in plant sciences... but that's not my world.

The trees and other plants I have known or worked with during my life, I have chosen to consider "natives"... or perhaps naturalized natives. They thrive in our part of the world and have become permanent fixtures in our local environment.

Landscaping of the kind we have fashioned is certainly not science, but it edges on magical. It begins with a combination of imagination, creativity, sensitivity, and in this case, unique collaborations. Add to this a sense of purpose, love of family and friends, and a deep appreciation for the art of the landscape and as well, the art in nature. It becomes something unexpected... and wonderful.

This is just a start:

Large Trees

• *Koelreuteria bipinnata*/Chinese flame tree. Native to China, Taiwan, Korea. Deciduous.
• *Podocarpus gracilior*/Sometimes called a fern pine. Native to East Africa. Evergreen.
• *Metrosideros excelsa*/New Zealand Christmas tree. Evergreen.
• *Platanus x acerifolia*/Sycamore tree. Sometimes referred to as a London planetree. Deciduous.
• *Arbutus* 'Marina'/Strawberry tree. Native to Ireland and southern Europe. Evergreen.
• *Olea europaea*/Olive tree. Considered a "naturalized native." Evergreen.
• *Cinnamomum camphora*/Camphor tree. Native to Japan and China. Evergreen.
• *Cupaniopsis anacardioides*/Carrotwood tree. Native to eastern and northern Australia. Evergreen.
• *Fraxinus uhdei*/'Majestic Beauty'/also known as evergreen ash and Shamel ash. Native to Mexico. Evergreen.
• *Bauhinia purpurea*/Purple orchid tree. Native of South China. Evergreen.
• *Tipuana tipu*/sometimes known as tipa, rosewood, or Pride of Bolivia. Native to Bolivia, widespread in South America. Deciduous.

Small Trees/Large Bushes

• *Euphorbia cotinifolia*/Copper tree or Caribbean copper plant. Native to Mexico, Venezuela, and Peru. In our climate, this is deciduous.
• *Cotinus coggygria*/Smoke tree a.k.a. purple smoke tree. Native to a huge area from southern Europe through central Asia, the Himalayas to northern China. Deciduous.
• *Cercidium* 'desert museum' or Desert Museum palo verde/Sometimes known as Parkinsonia Desert Museum. Native to Africa and Australia. Deciduous.
• *Caesalpinia gilliesii*/Desert Bird of Paradise a.k.a. Yellow Bird of Paradise and Barba de Chivo. This plant is native to the tropical Americas, mainly Argentina and Uruguay. It has been naturalized in Texas and is seen in many areas of the southwest United States. Deciduous.
• *Pyrus kawakamii*/Flowering pear tree. Native to the island of Taiwan. Unlike *Pyrus* of other varieties, this tree was granted its own species. The two we have are espalier.[21]

21 Chris Shea, email to Eloisa Haudenschild, 2017.

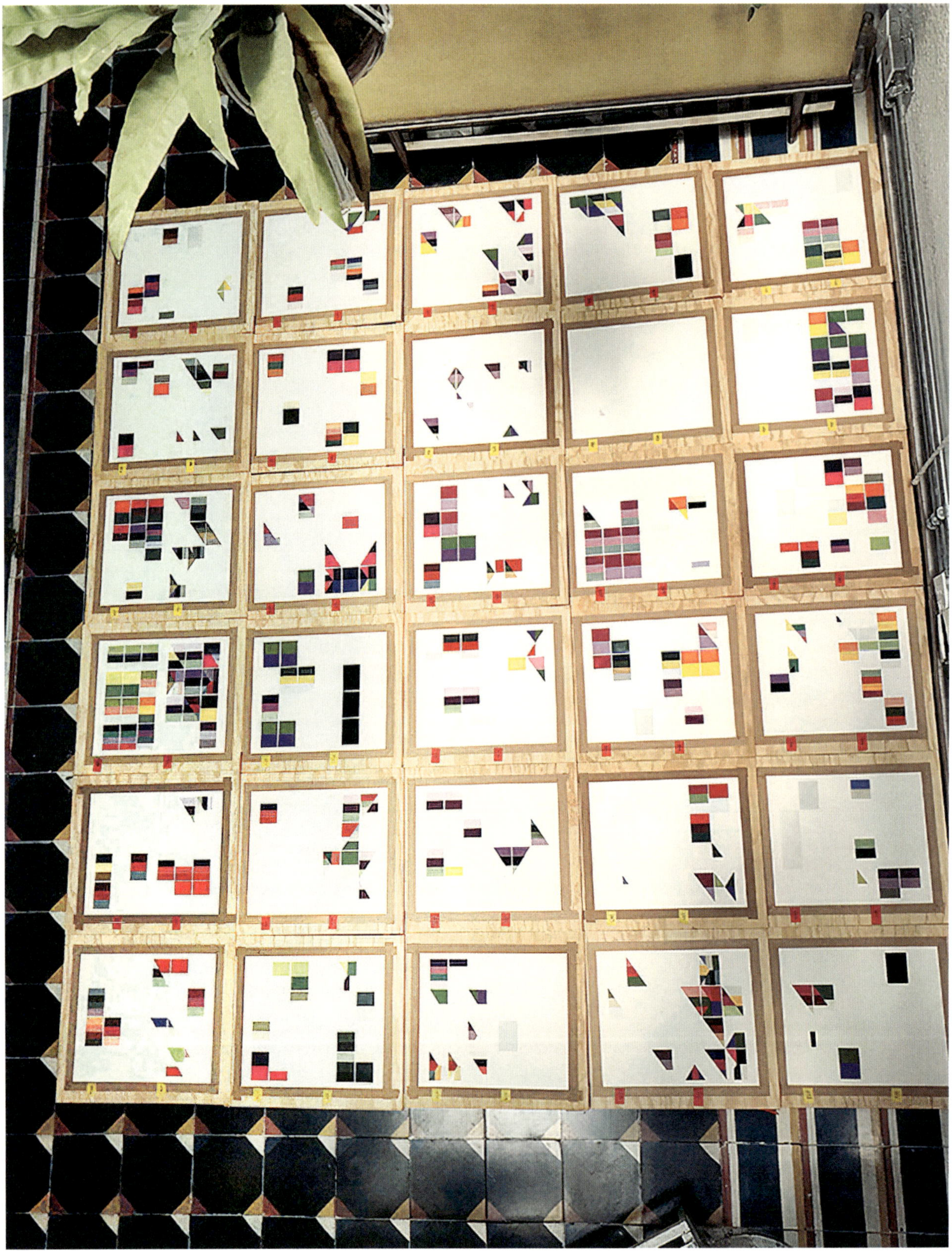

We saw each other many times over the next two years. We established a good relationship, although I confess I only met with him in his garden. I wonder what would have happened if we had met anywhere else. For instance, I never saw him inside the house. He considered the house and garden as equals, two elements that should be complementary, which is why he didn't see the need to enter the building.[22] "Is your house a mirror of the garden?" I ventured to ask on one occasion, to see if he would invite me to enter. After that, C began talking to me about his residence, based on what appeared through the window, to literally keep me outside. **"The closer you get, the more you see,"** he confessed to me.[23]

I decided to visit him in different seasons, perhaps hoping he would tell me about his new ideas and arrangements of the garden, or possibly because of my depression. **"And we can see the next generation down here getting ready to pop out. And here, you can see one of those beautiful accidents, while we are waiting for the other plant to bloom."**[24] Although he didn't want to speak with me about time, expectation was part of C as with any other gardener. "[I layer] perennial plants with grasses by the thousands," he said, "and the result is a progression of life that flows between the spaces in a plant bed, between the edges of time and, most powerfully, between the contours of [my] imagination."[25] "Might there be room for disappointment?" I inquired.

C frequently used to consider the past as part of a continuous present. As for me, I felt incapable of recognizing his prophecies or memories in this past-present. I had to get used to improvising from memory since time was a constant in our conversations. "The age of the realistic, imperishable, inexpensive, pollenfree, flexible, easily obtainable, socially acceptable, detergentwashable, artificial plant [is] here," he told me one day, out of the blue.[26] I thought, obviously, of the popularity of polyethylene. I can't even imagine C surrounded by artificial wisterias. He probably wanted to remind me of the importance of a living garden [I'm not sure of the importance of nature as such] to people's lives, using this botanical setting as the only possible space. That made me think of Chance the gardener. Or Chauncey Gardiner? In any case, we had never walked the city streets together, nor had we ever had coffee in front of a plastic planter, nor had he ever given me a flower bouquet. C didn't uproot plants until he had to. Nevertheless, he was an empathetic person—how could a person who enjoys taking the time to find out if a group of begonias is thirsty be anything other than empathetic?

22 Chakceel Rahen quoted in Sally Wilson, "Luis Barragán's Universal Garden," *The Planthunter* 16 (February 25, 2015). Web.

23 Shea, in conversation with Meyenberg.

24 Ibid.

25 Higgins.

26 "The Flowering Of Fake Flowers," *The New York Times*, August 23, 1964. Web.

And coldly the birch leaves are opening one by one.
Coldly I observe them and wait for the end.
And it ends.[27]

"I don't think so," said C. Time passes "and **you know, it's alright to touch plants.** That's how you realize they never get offended."[28] I was shy about touching plants. Or I plucked them while absent-mindedly walking down a path. Or, on the contrary, I avoided brushing against them (most of the time) for fear they would wither. This all had to do with my profound distance from them, my persistent mania for describing them in words. **"You can't be afraid to touch a plant,"** said C. **"Know what they feel like, and you can often tell if they're hungry or thirsty just by the feel of them."**[29]

C was an incredibly tactile person, and his hands took prominence in conversation. **I noticed he [had] a particular body language for touching each one of the different plants, a hand dance between forms, textures, sizes through the garden.**[30] Over time, I began to realize that C wasn't much of a talker. His voice could have been the result of my lack of attention or a mere sonic illusion. I began to imagine **a multichannel work, a sort of—recitative—chorus in the garden.**[31] I didn't pretend to translate his colors into my words, only to make a brief observation on the passage of time and the simultaneity of his garden's changing rhythms.

During the months of October, November, and December, I stopped visiting him. I assume he continued drawing in his notebook. Time, I feel, continued to wreak havoc on the garden and C. When I finally returned, I felt depressed and upset, and I asked him if he thought my depression had something to do with the change of the seasons. "It's unlikely," he said without paying much attention. "The percentage of the population affected by seasonal change is so small that I would discard it as a solid hypothesis. In fact, it's much simpler than that. You'll see, **this looks better with light against it,"** he told me, pointing to a remote section of the garden.[32] "It's all about the lighting, **a great light reflector."**[33] It's strange because I had heard him talk so many times about the change of seasons that I didn't question his authority. "Don't worry. I'm not going to abandon you to this. We'll have to continue evaluating the reason for all this uncertainty—but don't blame my plants."

27 William Carlos Williams, *Early Poems* (Mineola, NY: Dover Publications, 1997), 55.
28 Shea, in conversation with Meyenberg.
29 Ibid.
30 Email from Erick Meyenberg to the author.
31 Ibid.
32 Shea, in conversation with Meyenberg.
33 Ibid.

For everything, there is a season,
and a time for every purpose under heaven:
a time to be born, and a time to die;
a time to plant, and a time to pluck up that which is planted;
a time to kill, and a time to heal;
a time to break down and a time to build up;
a time to weep, and a time to laugh;
a time to mourn, and a time to dance;
a time to cast away stones, and a time to gather stones together;
a time to embrace, and a time to refrain from embracing;
a time to seek, and a time to lose;
a time to keep, and a time to cast away;
a time to rend, and a time to sew;
a time to keep silence, and a time to speak;
a time to love, and a time to hate;
a time for war, and a time for peace.[34]

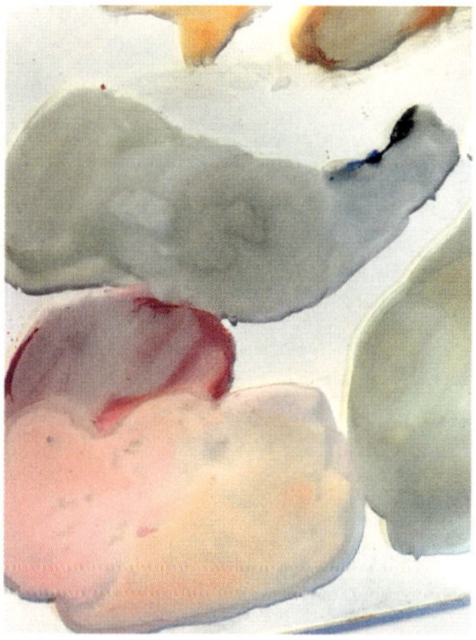

"In French," said C, "to be 'seasonal' means to be 'appropriate.'" That which is not seasonal refuses any relationship to time. "I don't believe things are consequences of each other. My experience," said C, "involves assembling groups simultaneously and seeing the result of these combinations. Results always come at the wrong time. The possibility exists of letting plants grow of their own volition and never to trim them, or simply let them perish without helping them to come back to life." C never stopped doing things in that garden, but he got annoyed when he was asked about withered plants.

The battle between beauty and non-beauty resembles a gardener's résumé. I think about all those things that escape our control, that cease to be in good condition and perish. "Like a corpse?" I asked him. "What happens when a bunch of flowers dries out?" He answered me with another question. I then realized that all of C's arrangements were about that period of decay and decline between late

34 Ecclesiastes 3:1–8 (American Standard Version).

September and early November.[35] I like plants and death as well. Dry plants help me remember that the garden is also a bit of nature. However, I don't think that the garden has to be something related to the landscape. Actually, the garden is a room where you enter and discover a certain intimacy.[36] When you cut down a plant because it's dry, it's because you want to see it gone. It's worse still if you want to cover the hole immediately.

"That sounds like a true metaphor for loss," I said, trying to cut him off. "Not at all," C said. "This is not death (the plants will regrow from the ground in the spring), but it is a decay [that] presents the garden at its most interesting.[37] People buy artificial flowers because they're afraid of death. People are unwilling to be at the mercy of a fading flower."[38]

At some point, I visited him unannounced. I think C didn't like my finding him outside, far from the garden. "Now then," commented C, taking up the conversation where we had left it a few months ago, "there are also parasitic seasons, those that make holes or pockets in time.[39] In a season like that, however often you come to visit me, you will never find me."

It was weird that C said "hole" and "pocket" as if they were synonyms. A pocket makes stuff disappear inside a coat but keeps it there—warm, playing around and moving in between fingers—until they re-emerge or fall apart and fuse with the fabric itself. It also causes surprise when you find something you thought you'd lost. A hole is something very different; things kept there can no longer be found. And perhaps that's the problem of voids and also my depression. I prefer to think that C is in this parasitic season, closer to a pocket—a season that could take the name of reading, music, lovemaking.[40] I want to think that is the reason we no longer speak. Another experience, a quite anachronistic temporal experience, generating around it more or less real and unreal spaces, fields of relaxation, fields of linguistically "amniotic" surrounds of nest or islands.[41]

I wonder, then, if these are the spaces C inhabits when he is not with me or scribbling in his journal—places without physical presence or work. Then I think he would be entangled in some other pocket, touching everything as he did with his plants. The question then arises, for C, whether I am in a pocket or a hole.

35 Higgins.
36 Ibid.
37 Ibid.
38 "The Flowering Of Fake Flowers," *The New York Times*.
39 Pascal Quignard, "La quinta estación," in *Albucius* (Los Angeles: Lapis Press, 1993), 55.
40 Quignard, 56.
41 Ibid.

Interestingly—and in spite of his refusal to indulge in lengthy descriptions—I can't stop seeing C's garden as a vast poem without words. In that journal of images, whenever there was an elongated segment of color, it looked like a syncopation within a musical score. If we think of the resulting segments as poetic feet (tetrameter, pentameter, etc.), [C's garden] could be scanned like a poem.[42] I took the trouble to arrange all the notes accompanying the lines by color groupings, leaving only the words. Perhaps this wasn't a very wise idea because the words again distanced me from the garden.

But C let me do as I pleased.

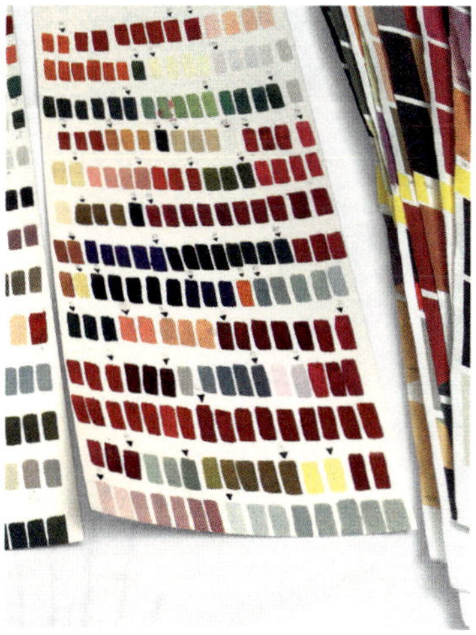

42 Paul Auster, "Black on White: Recent Paintings by David Reed," in *The Art of Hunger: Essays, Prefaces, Interviews, and The Red Notebook* (New York: Penguin Books, 1992), 400.

LANTANA GOLD MOUND

18

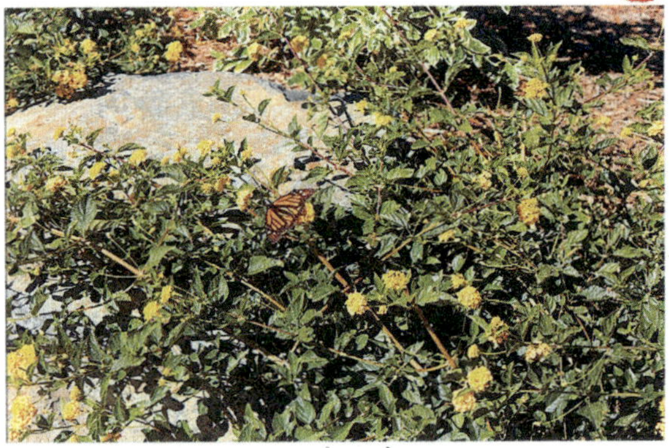

PITTOSPORUM TENIFOLIU
'SILVER SHEEN' PITTOSPO

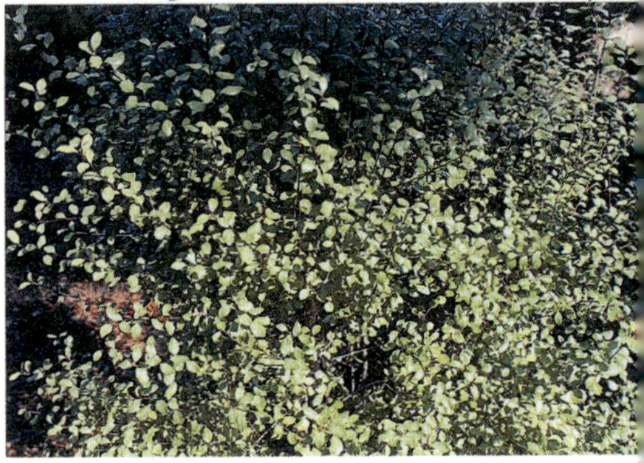

BREYNIA DISTICHA
(DWARF SNOWBUSH)

22

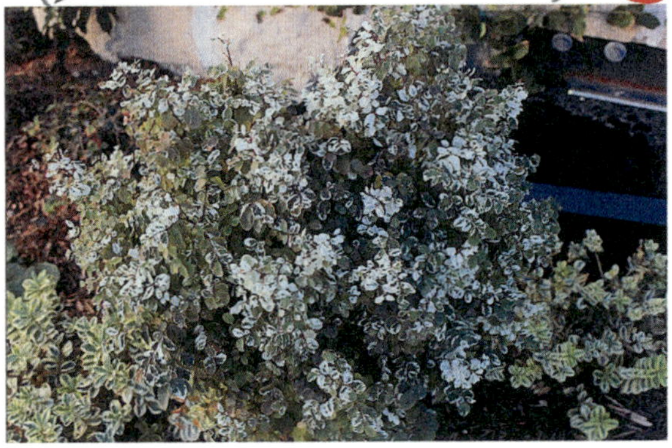

SILVER SHEEN P

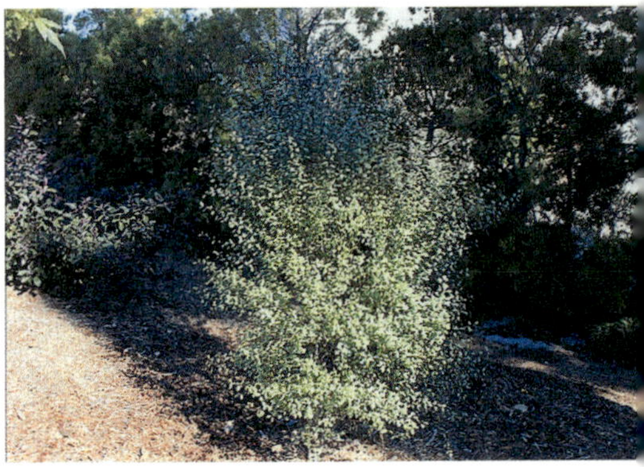

DWARF SNOWBUSH

HEBE

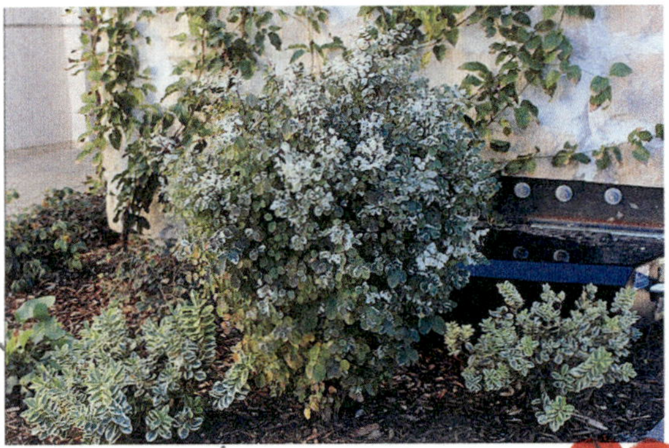

17 22

BREYNIA DISTICHA
(DWARF SNOWBUSH)

HEBE

LANTANA

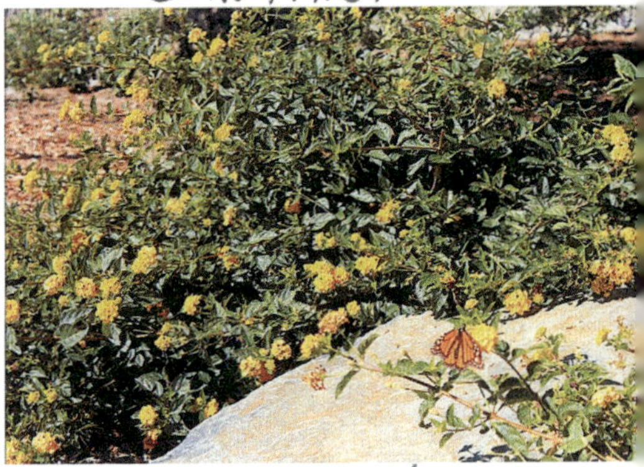

LANTANA
'GOLD MOUND'

COPROSMA 'PLUMB HUSSEY' (MIRROR PLANT) 20

BAUHENIA 'GALPINI' (RED ORCHID BUSH) 21

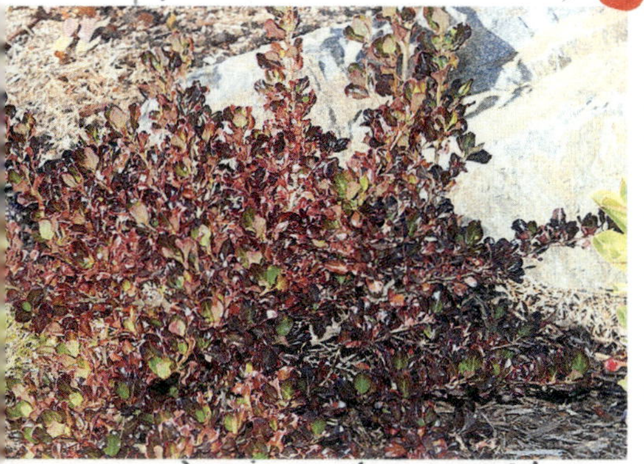

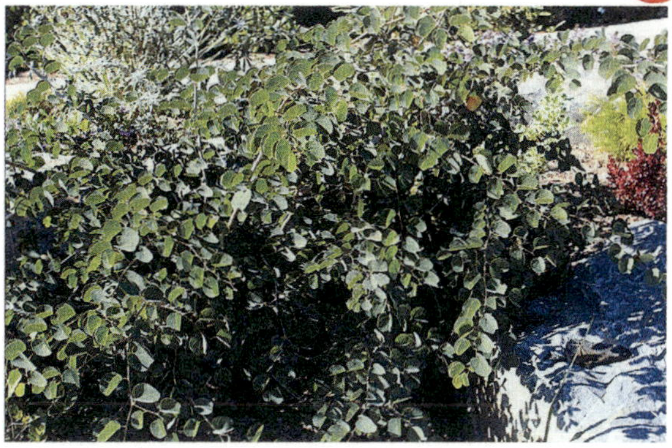

AESALPINIA GILLIESII (DESERT BIRD OF PARADISE)

BAUHINIA - RED ORCHID BUSH

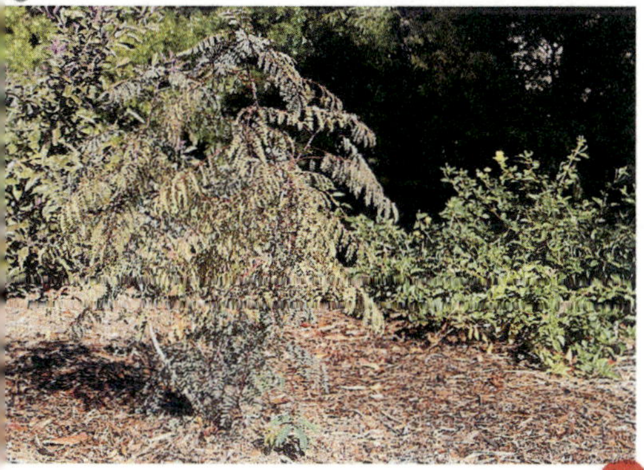

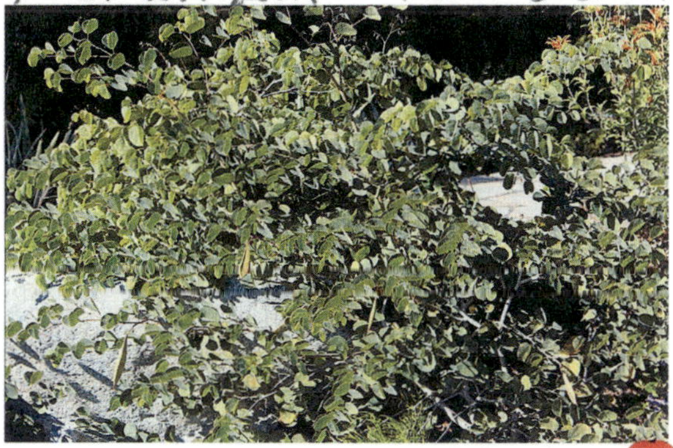

23

21

DESERT BIRD OF PARADISE

COPROSMA

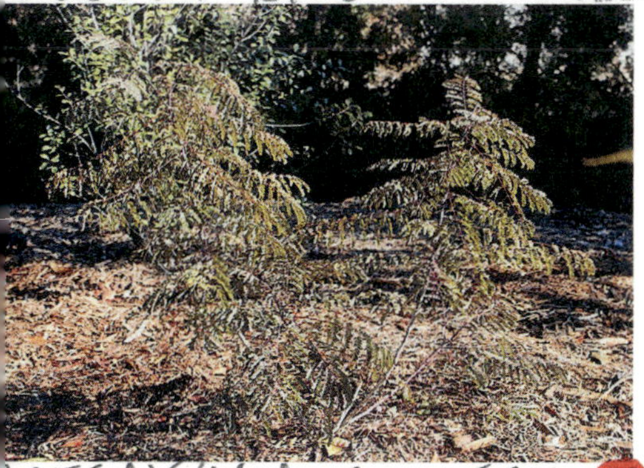

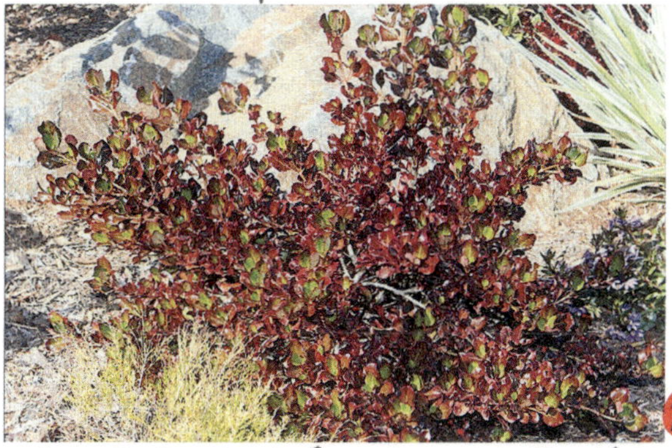

20

AESALPINIA GILLIESII 23

COPROSMA 'PLUMB HUSSEY' MIRROR PLANT

ICEBERG ROSES
&
STATICE (FOREGROUND)

37 7

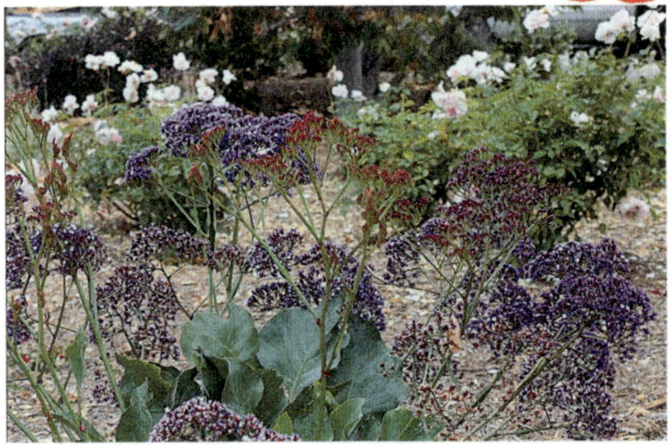

MINT MARIGOLD

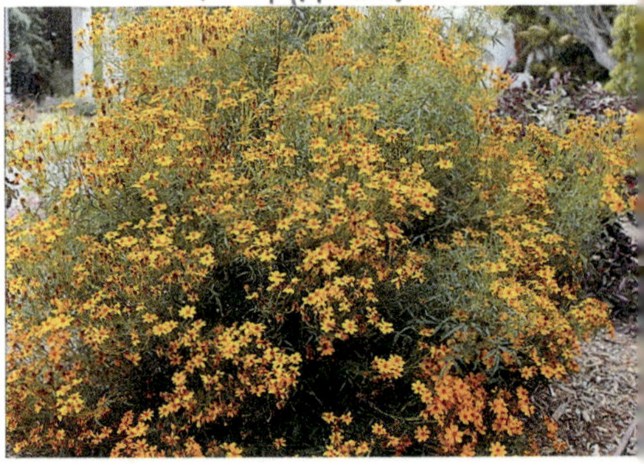

18 LANTANA (GOLD MOUND)

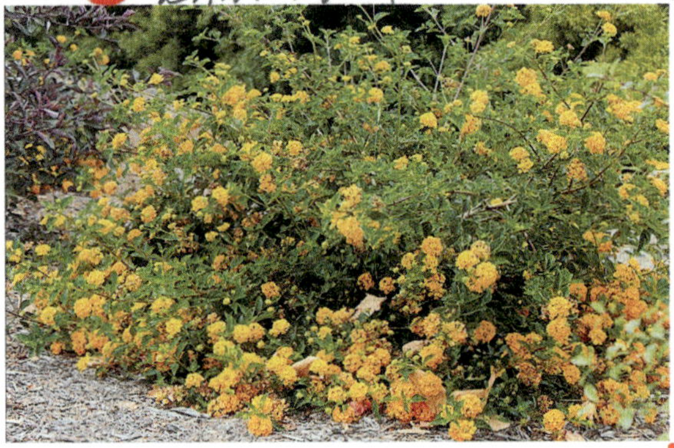

MINT MARIGOLD

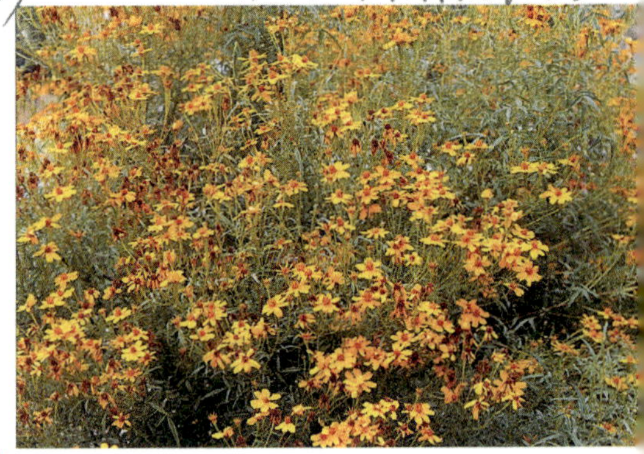

GOLDEN EDGE SKY FLOWER

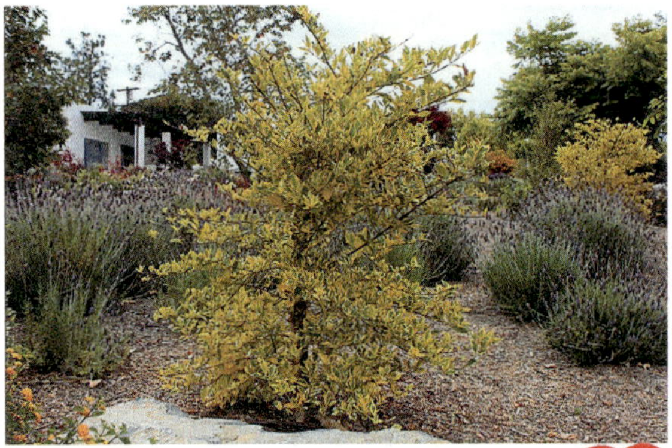

DURANTA
CENTER

16 24

FRENCH LAVENDER
BOTH SIDES

SCAEVOLA (WHITE

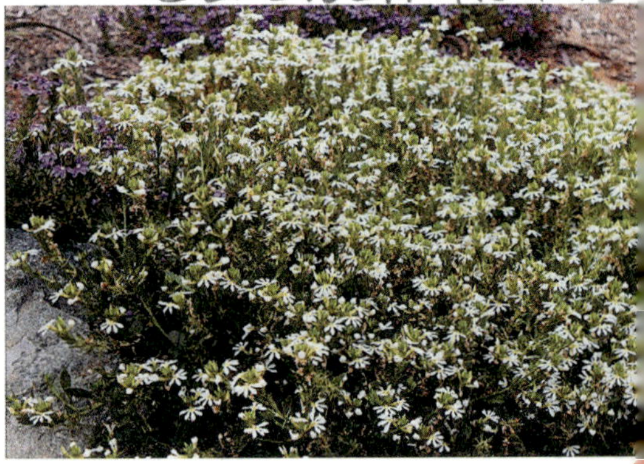

Ju

VITEX
'ARABIAN LILAC' 11

ICEBERG ROSES 37

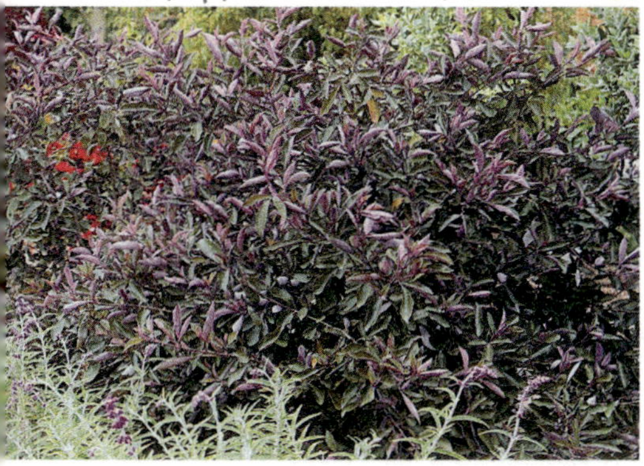

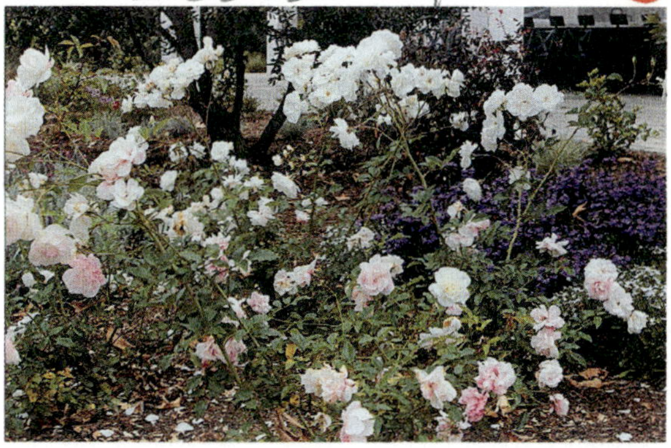

LIONS TAIL IN BLOOM

MEXICAN BUSH SAGE - SALVIA LEUCANTHA

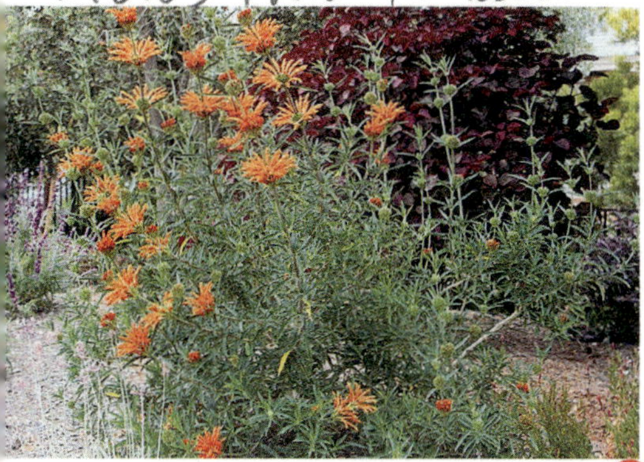

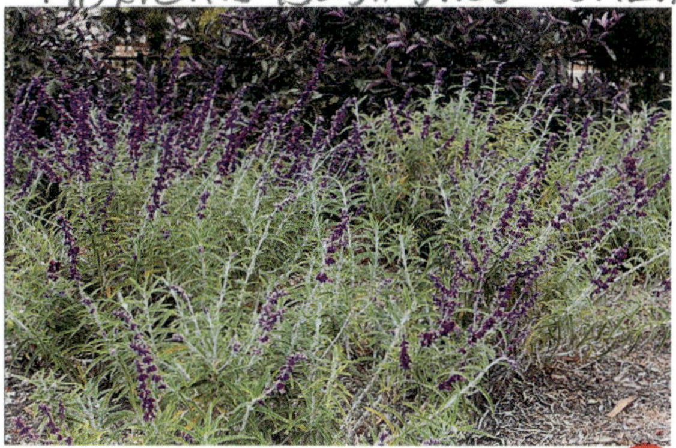

12

10

ITEX - 'ARABIAN LILAC'

"COPPER TREE"

CHINESE FLAME
LEAVES ONLY

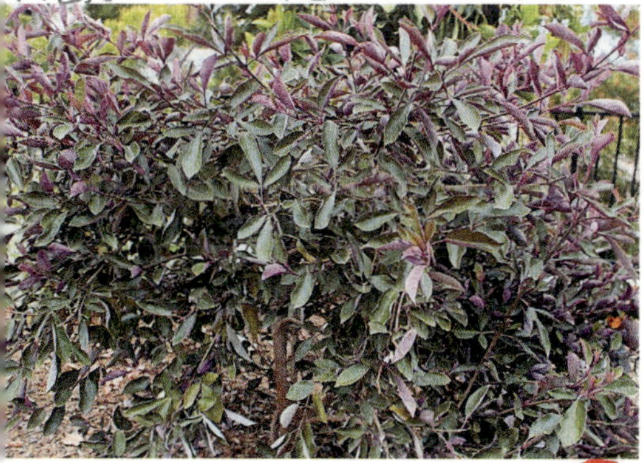

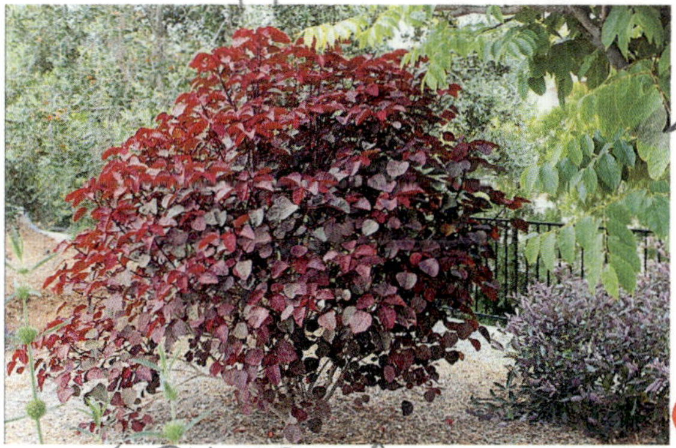

11

34

EUPHORBIA COTINOFOLIA
CARIBBEAN 'COPPER TREE'

2016

10

BUDDLIEIA - (BUTTERFLY BUSH)

COPPER TREE

47

DT

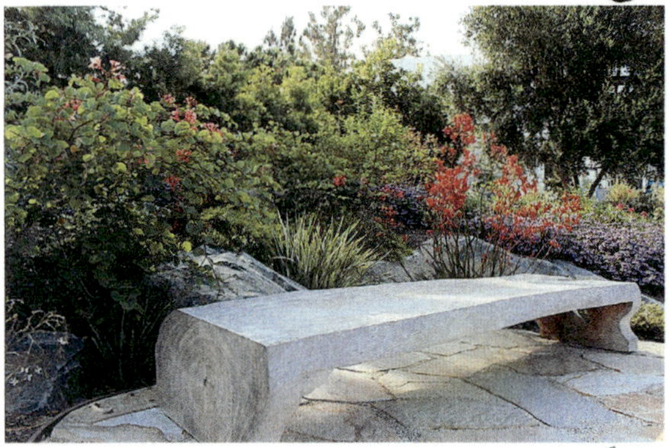

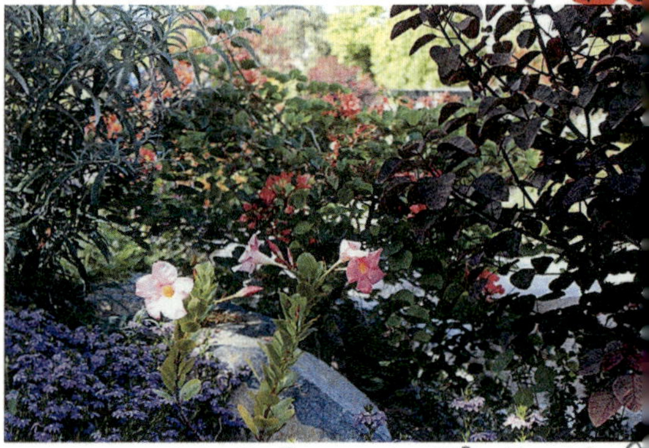

47 49 BUDDELIEIA BUTTERFLY BUSH → OLIVE TREE

27

BAUHINIA G. (FLOWERING) - KANG. P

BLUE SCAEVOLA MOST PROMINAN

DANIELLA

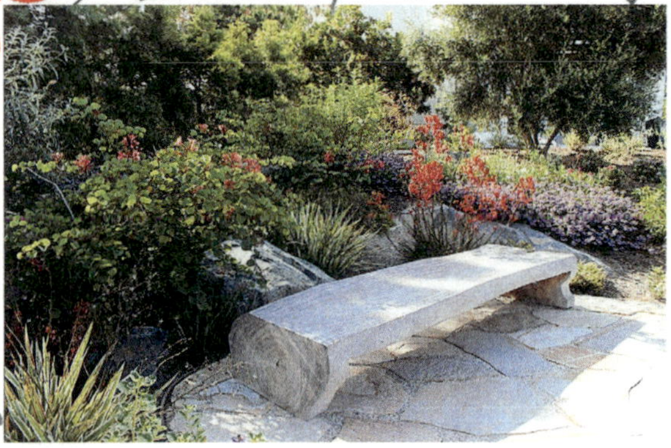

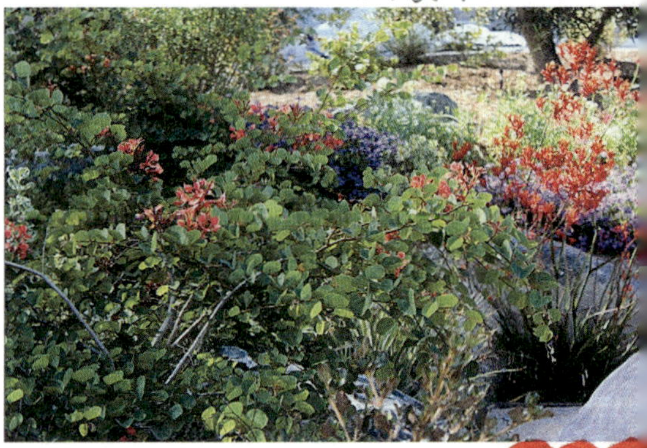

21 6 5

CENTRANTHUS RUBER

BAUHINIA G.

K. PAW

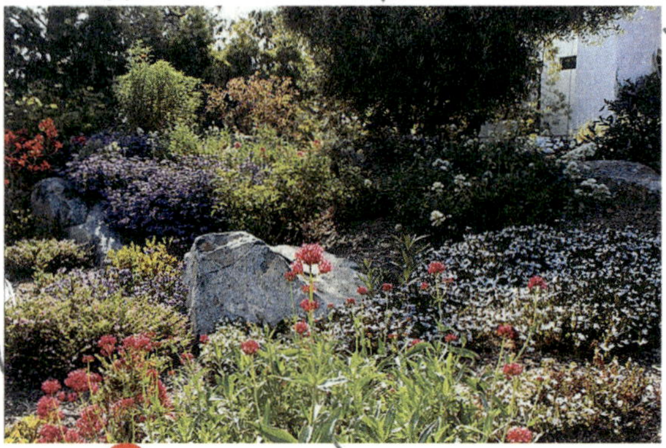

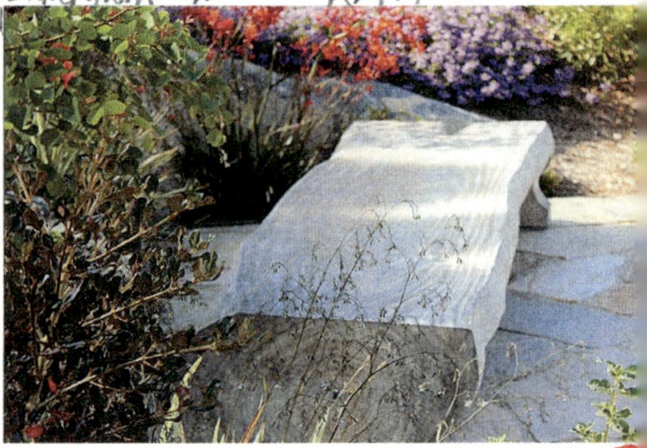

51

21 5

DT

CENTRANTHUS RUBER

AKA - RED VALERIAN

AKA - KISS-ME-QUICK

AKA - JUPITERS BEARD

WISPY STEMS

WHIRLING OR DANCING

WHITE GUARA BLOOMS A 1" A

…ST PROMINANT:
…AHINIA; COUSIN ITT-
…LUE SCAEVOLA

KANGAROO PAW YELLOW

SALVIA

21 32 6

49 8 19

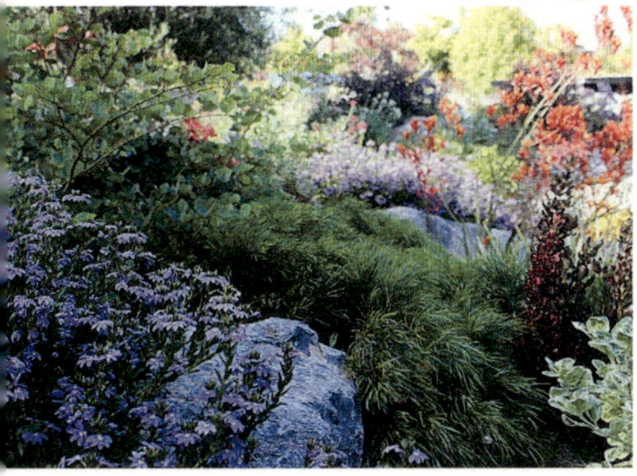

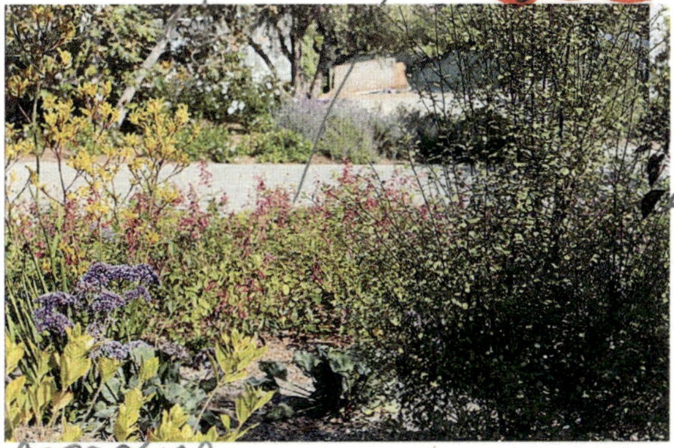

PITTOSPORUM TENEFOLIUM (SILVER SHEEN)

COPROSMA 'PLUM HUSSEY'

50 20 KANG. PAW RED

26

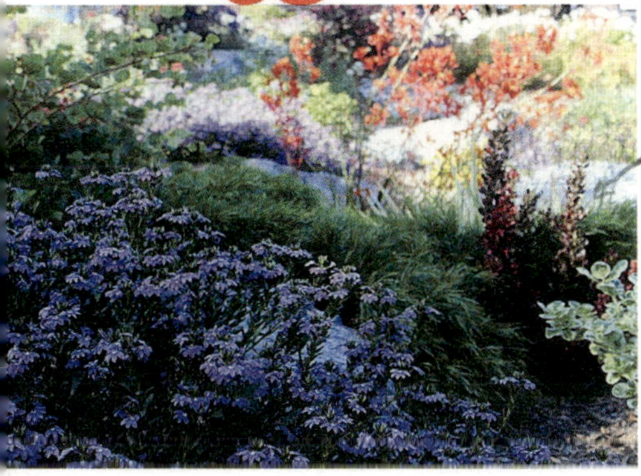

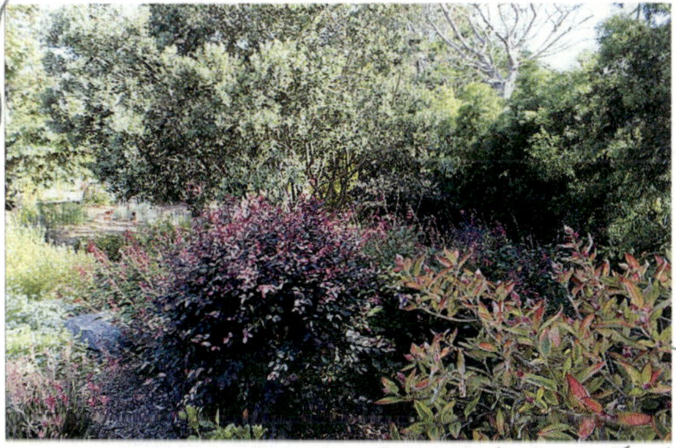

PRINCESS FLOWER

FLOWERING BAUHINIA G.

METROSIDEROS 'EXCELSUS'

PODOCARPUS GRACILIOR

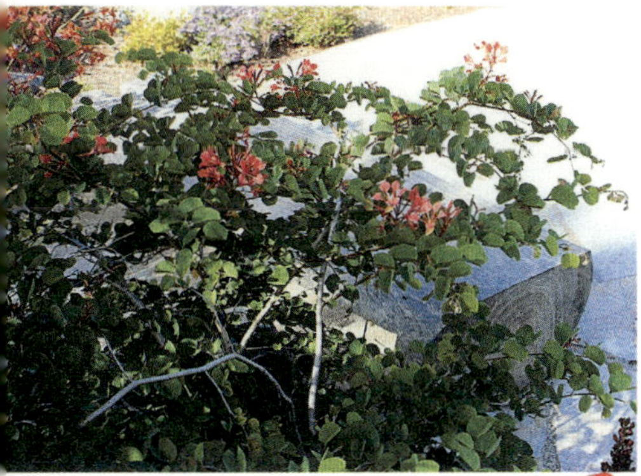

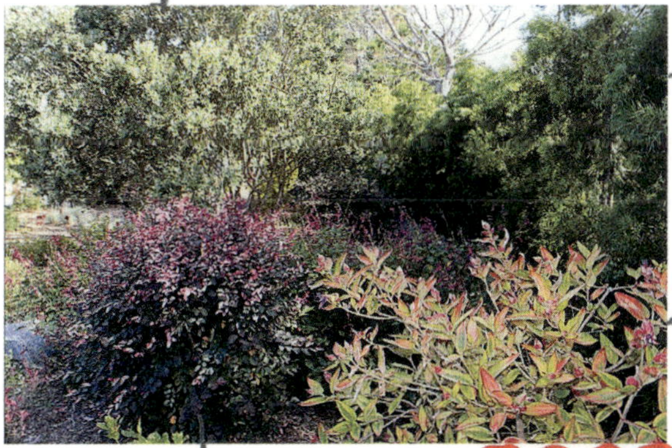

PRINCESS FLOWER

BAUHINIA GALPINI
RED ORCHID BUSH

21

43 52 29 26

BRENIA NIVOSA

MAJESTIC ALLUDES TO FLOWERS
SUPERB
…FLYS
BLOOM FROM PINK BUDS - LATE SPRING GUARA - GRK FOR PROUD

12

HEBE VERIGATA
VERONICA LAKE
17

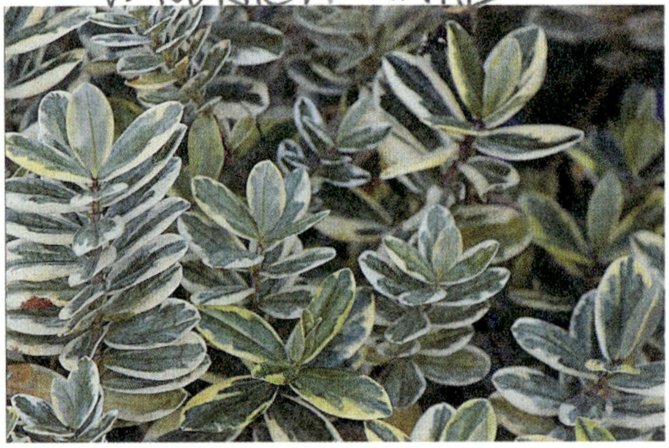

BAUHINIA G.
ARABIAN
LIL
6 21 11

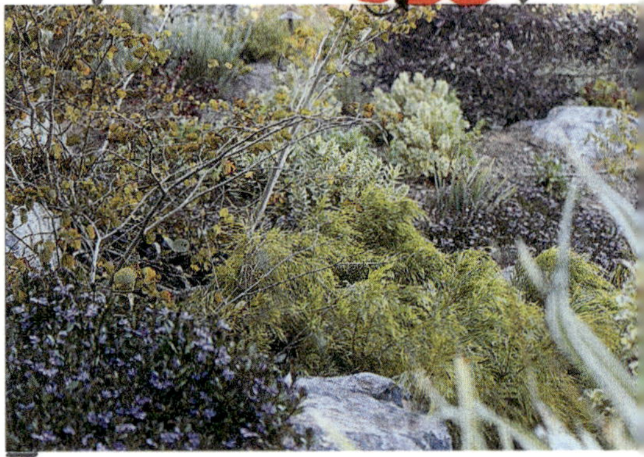

SCAEVOLA

HEBE

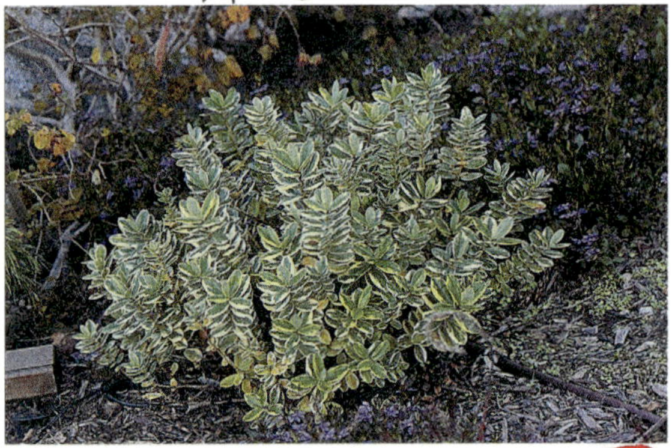

17

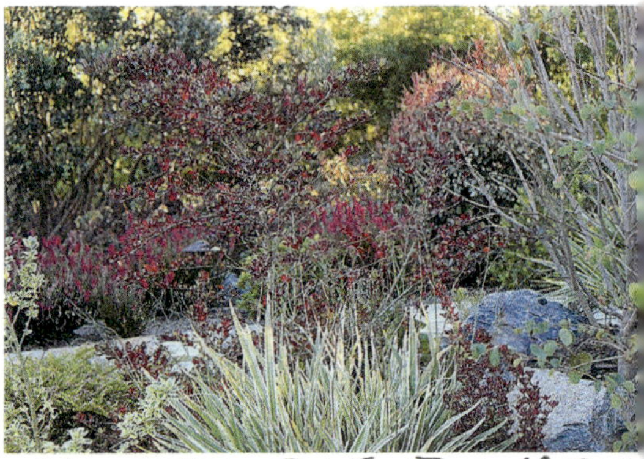

COLORFUL BLEND - VARIO

HEBE

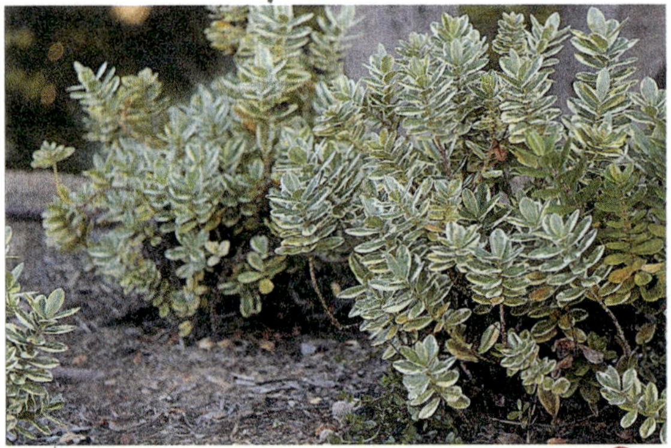

'HEBE VERIGATA
'VERONICA LAKE'
17

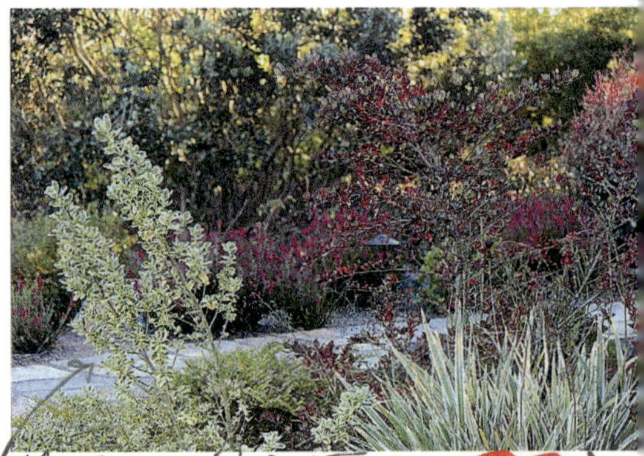

MIRROR PLANT,
'MARBLE QUEEN'
5 27

DANIELLA

METROSIDEROS
NEW ZEALAND CHRISTMAS TREE

DURANKTA V.

SMOKETREE

52 40 47

39 57

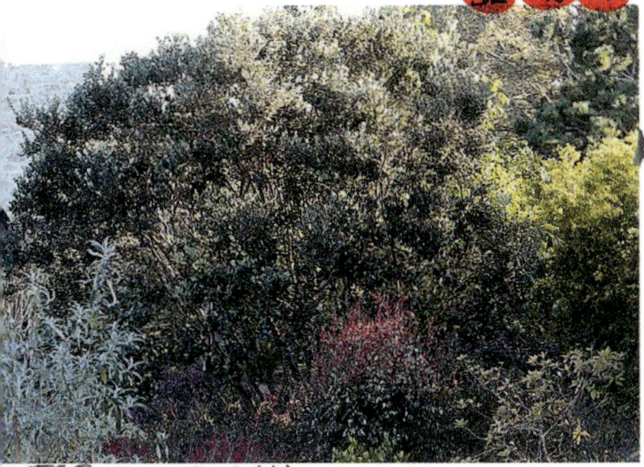

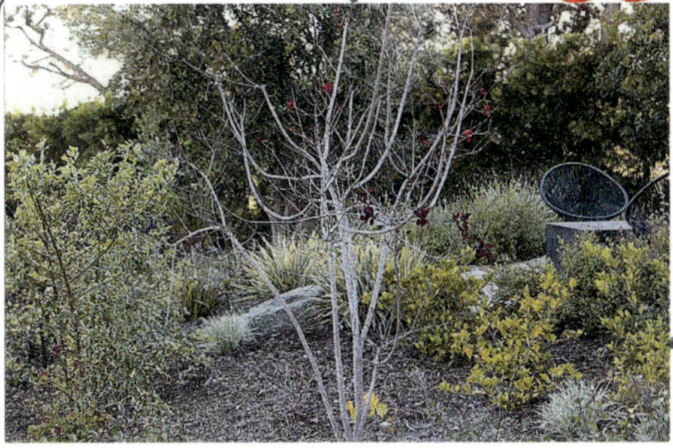

GARDENIA VECHII

…TTERFLY BUSH

KANGAROO PAW NEW FLOWERING RED/YELLOW

STAR JASMINE (BACKGROUND)

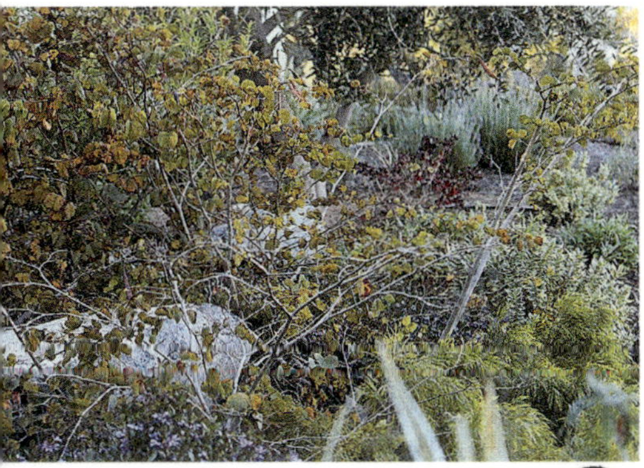

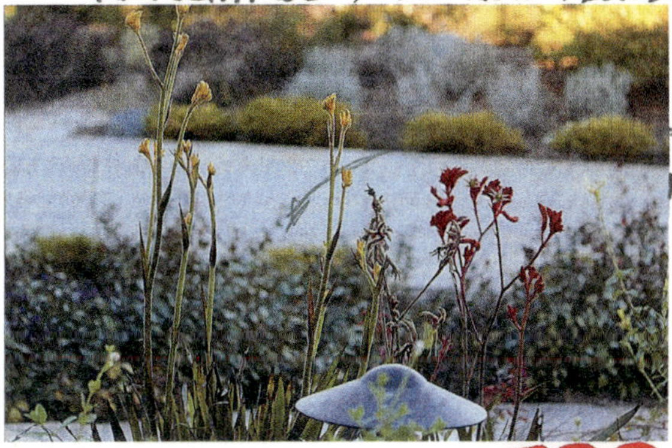

48 50 54

SYCAMORE

METROSIDEROS (NEW ZEALAND CHRISTMAS TREE)

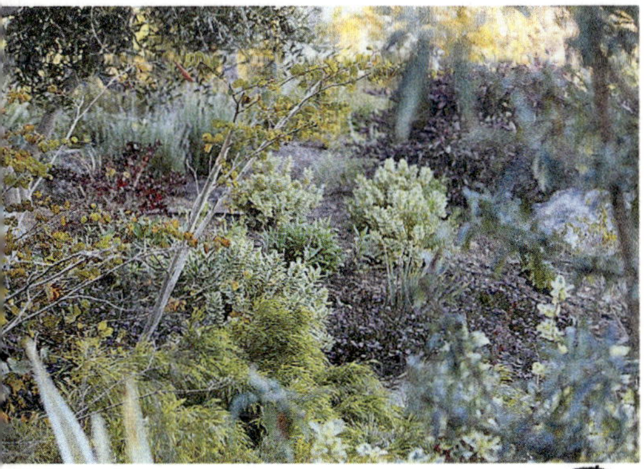

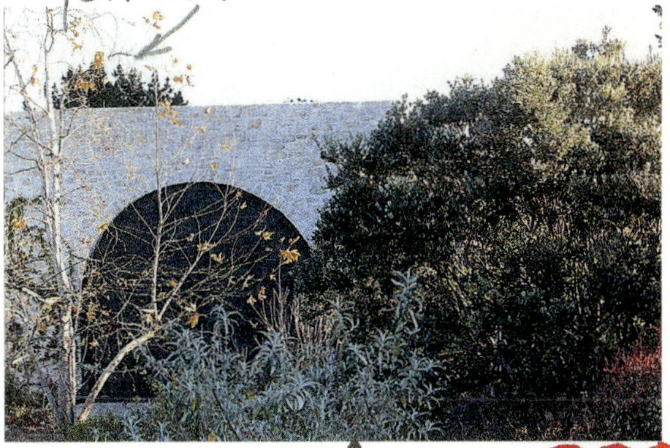

BUDDELIEIA (BUTTERFLY BUSH)

42 47 52

70

37

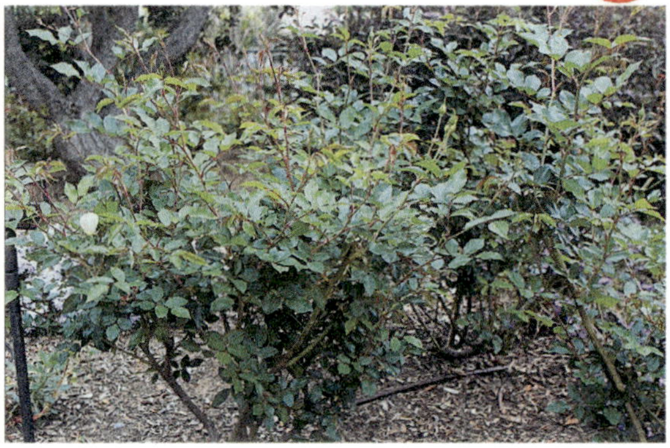

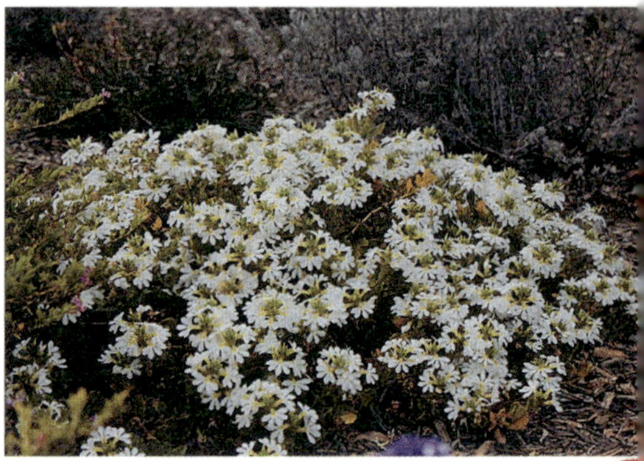

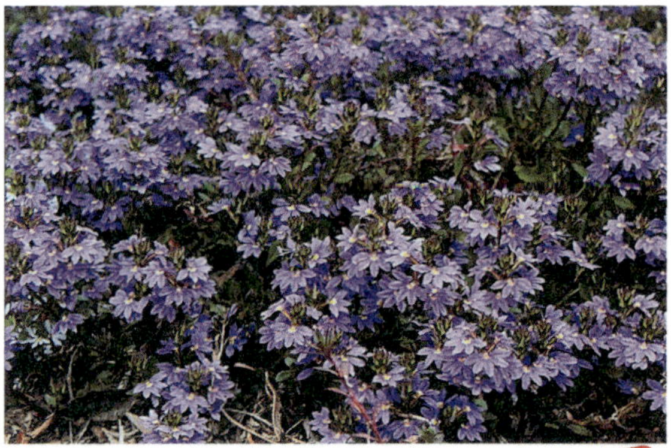

6

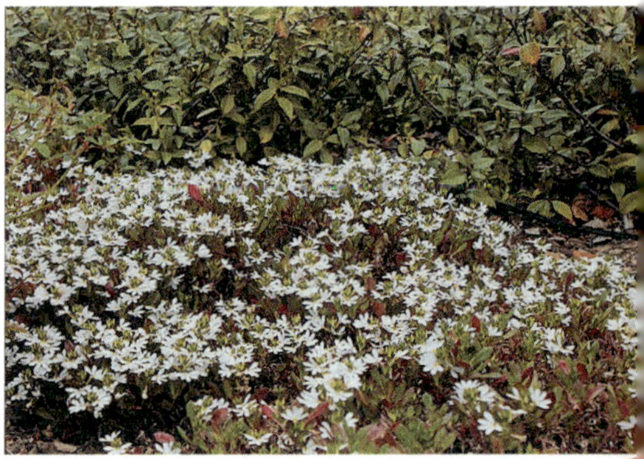

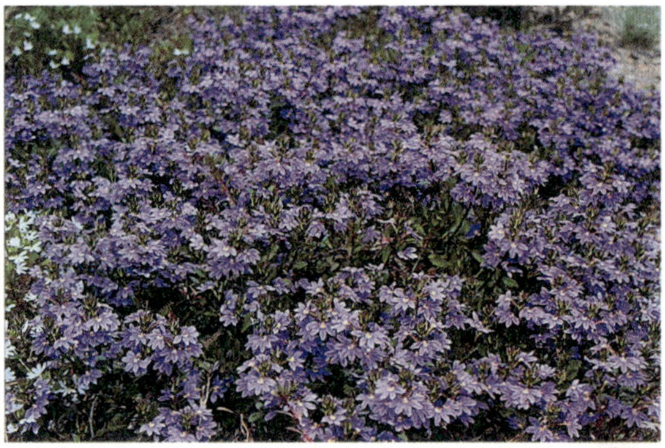

6

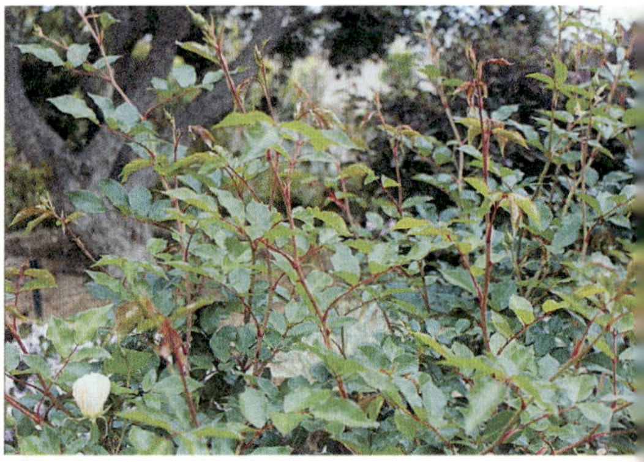

(SILVER ANOEK) 36

39

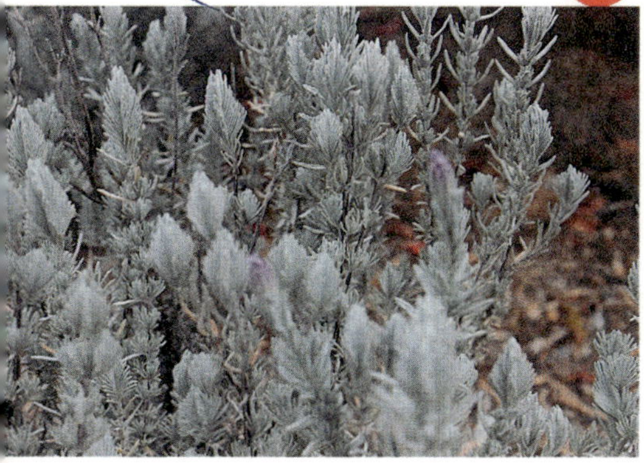

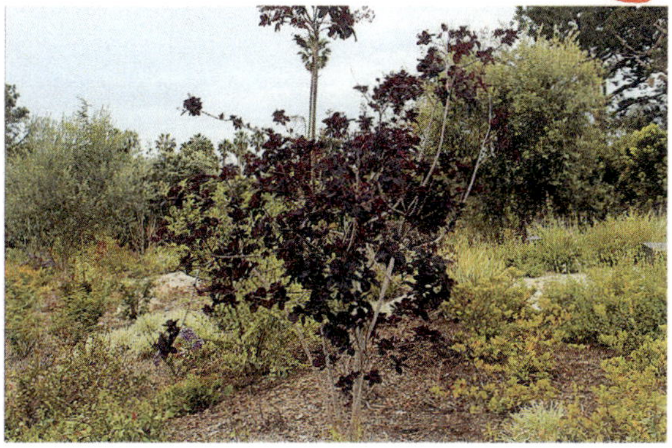

SILVER ANOEK

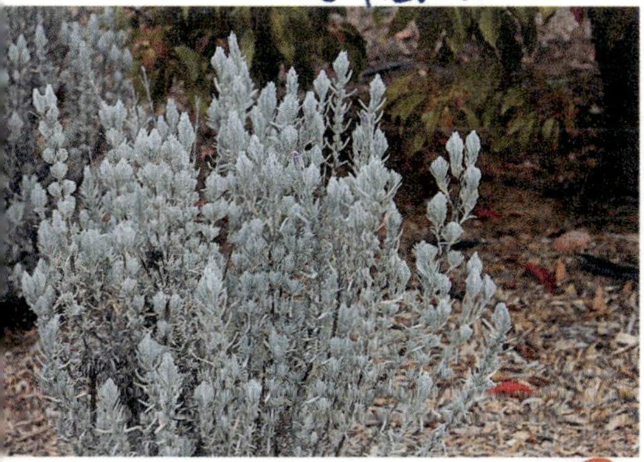

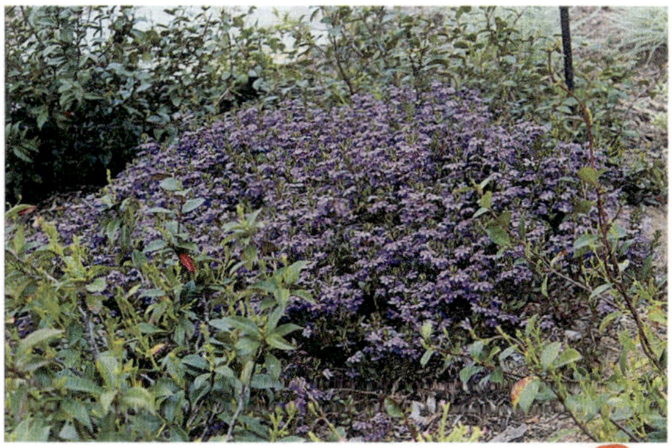

36

6

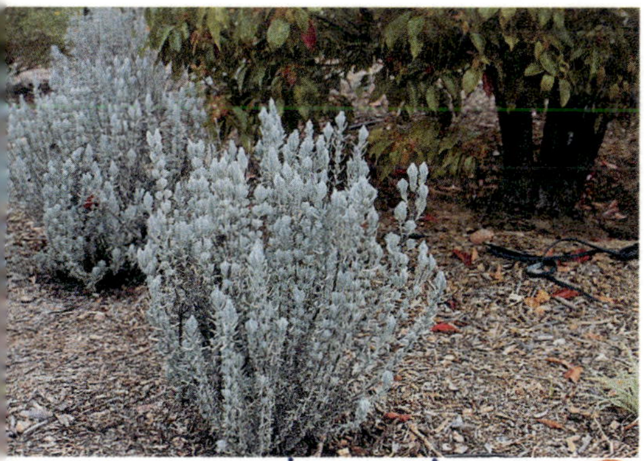

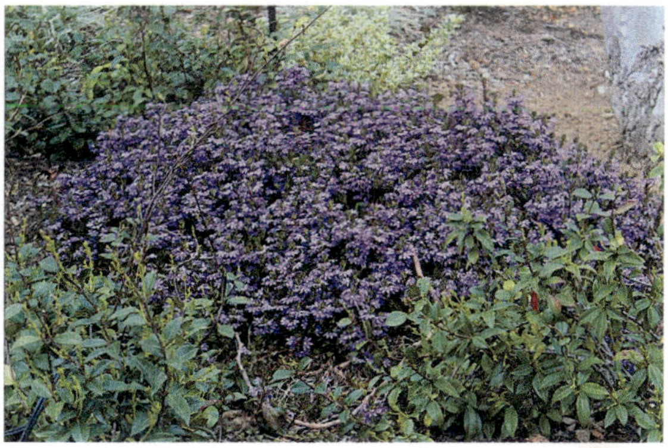

SILVER ANOEK. 36

6

74

RED: Red and white, rigid fiery red and orange / The new growth is red... the new stems are red and tiny, tiny green / The youthful red of a new leaf, spotted amongst the chartreuse leaves / This is just indescribably red and green and... / Real spikes of red and green, the new growth of the red leaf / Blanket of red and fuchsia and dots of white and green and red tinged leaves / Surrounded by these deep velvety reds / Even red stems beneath / Again with those red veins / And the flowers are ugh something of a brick red or even a coral color / That bright red is just... it's like a... / This one has the reds and pinks and greens and very glossy, almost varnished / And new growth red stems / And the flowers become red and white / This is just coming from this cold season, so it has lots of red and some of its natural green, but this is going to bleed and blend pinks, and light greens and even some white / Just some very deep reds and pinks, and you can even see that this one has some white or cream in it / How many shades of red and copper are there? / And there is some of that red in it again / Or solid red? / There's a red and it'll have a little hint of yellow or orange in them too / And this one got the red, a little bit of the almost burgundy and yellow and orange / You know, it goes from the red face to the blue and then the whites / Sort of a reddish stripe / More dramatic when they are fully red / So many plants have that, you know, new growth with that red in it, you know / Big red / It's a spectacular red, very deep and velvety / It's a really, really unusual fuchsia, red... I'm not sure what to call it / Burgundy red over a cream color / They start with this red and then they will turn green / This is one that tricks you, it has the red coming up and then it sprouts that bright, bright yellow / This is a burgundy / You know they just spring out in a red or really in a deep, deep burgundy sometimes and pinks / Can you see how the sun comes in behind it and the reds and the oranges / As the other is going to return to a red / But the new growth is red / New growth looks red / Nature's bouquet, a perfect arrangement of red and green / The red and white of the salvia, almost smiling / An umbrella of red / Spikes of impressive red / Some new growth, the red and green / Velvety cover, red / Very deep red, there's even a variety that's black / Here's some really, really red down here / Original Jupiter's Beard with a red / But up on the top you can see how much bolder the reds are or the coppery-red is / We can see some new very red right there / Some deeper reds in it, not so orangey / With the redder color on the back and then that flower / Of course it gets that reddish cast to it and it becomes a very green leaf, these are very green, but they start out like this, even the stems are red / That lilting look of the new leaf on this, with the red and the light green / The stem of it just looking red / We will probably find some few spots where the leaves have turned red, you can see how they start / And sometimes it's just completely crowned with red / The leaves on these get really red. WHITE: Accents of white / It's a velvety white / A white spotted with green and grey / You know, every one of those light white / It's a white flower / This will turn almost completely white with just spots of green / White playing with the light / Some undescript, certainly dwarfed by the radiance of the white / Sitting on top of the white to grey stem / But we call it white, it likes to bleed a little bit of lavender sometimes so you can see that small flower / And the white has a really pretty contrast to it / Or the white edges of an aging yellow / There's no matching the softness of this white / But it's just that pristine white / Sometimes white is the most elegant color / Soft white / Almost white at times during the year and has just that grey / And it exposes this white / It's a white cone / Flotilla of white, bright white / Both white and pink / The white trailing Lantana / Nice bright white flower occasionally little dots of purple in it, the roses blooming / Layers of white and shadow, each layer shadowing or shading the next layer / Some of them out in the sun will pick up almost a white. CREAM: And cream / Cream and green in the background / Creamy colored and brown even greens shades of green / And a new cream color / Even a little edge of cream, it's a very, very happy yellow / Pretty color cream and yellow and pink. ORANGE: Shades of orange / An orange over green reaching out toward the sky / A bright orange / So it's got the oranges and the reds that we have looked at on another one / So, I don't know how orange or yellow it will end up / Just on another side of the tree and they're more of an orange color / This is the orange one that is not doing anything right now / And this one is an orange one / I'm sort of enjoying this look of this reflection of the back side of this orange and yellow tall / The orange of the Kangaroo Paw up there / It's got the orange and yellow in it / When it flushes out completely it may be all orange. YELLOW & GOLD: Yellow with green spotted / It's the Goldmound Lantana / Yellow bells / Eye-catching yellow with a hint of lime-colored green / That slippery pale yellow and light green, just awakening / A confusion of yellows and greens spotted with reds and rust / Soon to be yellow / And some young yellow / Vibrant yellow grading the sun and reflecting it, bright and beautiful... (oh... supposed to be doing just colors) lined with red / Sunlight yellow / An aged yellow, turning white / Smiling glow of yellow and purple and lavender, cream and green in the background / Our mint marigold / Eye-popping yellow and red / The golds, and the greens, and the yellows / A light lemon yellow / A bright sunny yellow with kind of a smile of red and a flower of yellow and faint grey-green, even a little edge of cream / A light yellow / Bold yellow / That softy yellowish / Radiant yellow / And once that opens up, that's when you get the yellow flowering coming out / The colors in this, you know, as they are coming out of the winter cycle are a little yellow, but they come back to this, again just to a kind of a very / Tiny yellow flower will pop out / You can't get over the bright yellows and then this bold bright red / We have kind of a combination of yellow, orange / Amber glow / You see, it's maybe a little bit of an amber or it's going to turn into an amber color / But they do look like gold medallions floating on top of the plant / Your eye wanders through that bright yellow there and it makes you look / It's interesting again to see how yellow some of them can be / Just the difference in color in yellows / Just look at how different it is in the shadier areas, how hot the yellows are on the sunnier areas / Eye-popping, bright, happy yellow color in the back / Some of the older leaves have a darker yellow / Possibly an amber / There's nothing fresher than a yellow / And it sprouts this bright, bright yellow / Two different varieties of the yellow / And just the yellow / Little yellowish kind of a flower, but you can't tell till it opens up, you can see the yellow around it but it looks like it might even be a purple / The yellow; a little bit / And if you look closely, it's almost a yellowish throat that it has / Sometimes I just wonder if it's a reflection of the green / Getting hit by the elements, it's a little bit yellower, but they'll green up and they will get more upright / But you can't help to look at them, because they have that little yellow dot, that says: I'm right here / The deep yellow, the variegated and the other one / There's almost like a limey, creamy color. GREEN: Variegated green, bleeding into / Glossy green / Glossy and bold green / Glossy green tinged with yellow and pink and cream colors / The light and dark effects of the grassy green colors / Variegated greens and creamy white, dark green, light green / Deep green, glossy / The sunlit greens and shadowed greens / A unique shade of green, wrapping these soon to be flowers / Shiny glossy greens, chaotic spots and blots of green and cream / A collaboration of green with red and purple and yellow / Glistening green, glossy and dull / Shades of green, light, dark shading into brown / A mossy green / Green lines, looking like a current river, a river of green / Sharing with the green, sharing the green with the red and the purple / And green and grey and green-grey / Fern green... with a lighter chartreuse / Embracing the greens and yellows and purple and lavender around it / The older growth of the green tinged with red or amber / Surrounded by shades of green / Pale green stark / Light green, dark green / Leaves medium green with a grey bottom / It is green, pink, red, purple / And sometimes it's just green, almost / The new growth in the greens, pinks and purples / A grey-green or even a deeper green top and a grey felt-like bottom, soft looking stems / Green stems and red / The color I call chartreuse / A future of chartreuse, lime, a limey kind of green / Beautiful deep green and light green / Shades of dark green / Soft and light green / Darker green on top, but really just a medium green / Grey greens and yellow veins / And it has a very rich, small green leaf / You know, it will tease you with a really deep green leaf too / Greyish green on the bottom and from a distance you'll see a lot of a grey-green / Where you have a multitude of greens / You can really have that glossy shiny green too / And it always has a hint of a kind of a limey or yellow green / Don't have a real good name for that green, it's somewhere between a grey-green and almost a blue-green / This variety has a little bit lighter green in the leaf and a white / It's almost like splattered with green / Just deep green and very lush / Green and strong / With that nice green / This great green trunk / It filters your view as you look through to very green things and it gives a really colorful aspect to the garden / It's almost a shadow of color over the green / This is primarily green, a little bit of color around the stark / The green underbelly here / And for a time even this is a delicate kind of a green and soft looking / And then this pops up out of this green shield / This has a lighter, much lighter green too / But it's reeling, and some of it is going back to that original green / And yet they green out / See this deep green down here / Very new, very green / The leaves are almost a lime green around the green against that yellow, and they just bleed green / And then you get those few that just refuse to turn green and just stay yellow / So it's mostly green and then ... boom! / Just kind of a basic green and great for shade / A canopy of flowers over this green plant / These leaves are much greener, these low leaves they are just a beautiful deep green and glossy / So you'll get more green, but less flowers / Sometimes I just wonder if it's a reflection of the green / Larger leaf, little greener / Again here you see how nice and green these are and are hanging out in the shaded area / But it's sort of a chartreuse color / Lighter than that deep green when they get older / Twenty different colors of green / Fifty shades of green / The various shades of green on the top / Green if you pull it this way, purple if you pull it that way / Is it a green stem or is it an orange stem? / All green up to here and then here's the flower coming up, and you can see the orange in its throat here in its neck / Dry green. BLUE: The blue spotted with white / Soon to turn this blue / Shades of blue / The blue and the bright but dainty white / These tiny blue and yellow flowers / This is called Blue Dianella and again it's got that blue flower /

But it does definitely bring out the blues / We call it blue because it has a blue hint to the green-bluish, purply kind of flower and then the little white / And it looks good with the blues and the purples and the whites / This has a blue spire, it's a blue salvia / Deep blue spires, very inviting to look at / Dripping off the tree, the blue Sky Flowers they call them / It is unbelievable, it's almost an indigo / It is the richest blue with this, again, kind of a chartreusey sort of a leaf / Just a blue that is almost impossible / And as it grows out it fools you and it gets that indigo color / You know, almost an florescent kind of blue / You just don't get the blue and the purple and the yellow hearts here, the stems have red in them / You know, every version of the Sky Flower is blue. VIOLET: It's a lavender trumpet / Purple spire / Lavender petals / Spires of purple and blue / A shining purple / Lavender cream and yellow, tinged with purple tips / Striped with a light, light purple, maybe red / The early color of purple and green / The growth of purple and green and rust and red / A nearly inconceivable combination of purple and green... and green, and green and purple, light and velvety / The inviting lavender / The lavender of lavender / Deep dark purple / With a lighter purple / Near lavender, like the lavender / Deep purple, tiny, tiny flowers / Lavender and a grey / If you see the purple side and the green side of the new growth / Twirling purple of the new growth / With its fringe of hairlike... purples, the reds / Small purple flower, seems so shy / Just a spire of purples and whites / There's been a wake up call for the purple spires / Such a dark, dark purple at the beginning / Purple or blue or purple and white, blue and white / Or sea lavender color? / Or you look at it and think: This is going to be a purple flower / It starts up with these purple edges / We get these purples / Lavender flower / Sort of a purple color / When you look closer at these, the purples bleed as if you've painted them with watercolor / The deeper lavender here and then it bleeds to the center of each one of the petals / And it turns to a sort of a mauve color / From deep, deep purple, it changes to orange and rusty colors / When the white pops out of the purple / The new growth has that purple kind of a look and then turns green, but not always / A nice mix of purple and green and a fuzzy kind of a flower / As it grows up, you can see that the purple is the new growth / And some of it will stay purple, and some of them will turn into a very deep green, but it's sort of a flat green, it's not a really glossy plant / But it's kind of a combination of this dainty lavenderish pink kind of a flower and then a little bit more of a rigid leaf / Really pretty purplish flower / And this one is really starting to flush out that purple / Small leaves, just deep purple / And you can see how the shades of the lavender... change / But that deep purple, you know, and it lightens up in here / And it's just a deep, deep purple / Bluish lavender, dripping strings of flower / And that... I just have to call it purple on the bottom / You see that purple. PINK: A vibrant, vibrant fuchsia / Subtle pinks and quiet greens / The pink and purple strings of color / Translucent fuchsia or red / Kind of a sweet little pink there / And it's a really special color, it's a fuchsia / And this is the pink one / It's a very sweet flower, very pink, very feminine looking / Just really draws the light and the pink really stands out, really beautiful plant / It will get some pinks and some yellows and kind of reddish colors, but ultimately it turns very white / You know, a very, very light pink / You'll get a couple of flowers that have that pinkish just all around the leaves / And then we have some pink ones too, that haven't come up yet / Just looks like a bit of a dull kind of a fuchsia color and then it shoots out this beautiful flower. GREY & SILVER: The light grey, almost white effect of the bottom side of these leaves / The light grey with an almost white in the sunlight with a grey-green mixed in / Grey at the borders / Grey and brown holding up the color / Light grey, felt-like texture / Grey / A grey / A dry rigid grey wrapped in cream / The grey and deeper purple of this lavender / The faint greenish grey color of the stalks / The grey and green and purple / A little bit of a dirty look to its grey / Sort of a dusty look to them, but the grey is different / Kind of a grey, the green on the top and the grey / Compared to the older leaves on it, you know it turns really an interesting grey / You see the old growth on the trunk, you know, the grey, brown kind of a look / But there are more greys in the trunks than anything / Lavender, it's a grey lavender / This is a grey or a grey-green, yeah / And this one over here, that's more grey. BLACK: In particular, it's called Black Knight / It's just perfect rings of black, yellow and white / If you see it, in a way, there's... it's almost black... and, as it grows out, it fools you, and it gets that indigo color / With edgings of black in it. BROWN, RUSTY, COPPER: The copper and purple / The subtle rusty color, the subtle rusty leaves against the purple leaves / Sprawling threads of brown and green, interlaced with glossy deep dark green and yellow / Whether brown from age / Wounded brown surrounded by green / A really firm brown bark / Browns and greys / Kind of moves into some browns and reds and greens, it's got a lot of color, a lot of life to this plant... it really shows, it really picks up light / Rusty sort of a color there, I guess / A little bit of brown is there / The bottom side of the bark is very brown, and it'll stain it for a while / I always expect a tree to look like... brown![43]

43 Shea, in conversation with Meyenberg.

The garden was different, less cared for. The sun was still there, to be sure, and light temporarily covered up the neglect. C had stopped cultivating the plants he loved because he couldn't precisely remember their names. He let chance determine the selection of species. He still preserved a memory of the color spectrums and seasonal cycles; he could not dispense with that structure that allowed him to go on living. The garden was full of circumlocutions, something not at all common, whether for the garden or for C. He had lost initiative and didn't seem interested in having a conversation. His vocabulary had become unintelligible and the garden unrecognizable. Is there a way in which a garden cannot be read? If it hadn't been for the memory of past conversations, or the years prior to our first meeting, I would probably have understood nothing. That's the problem when one communicates with words.

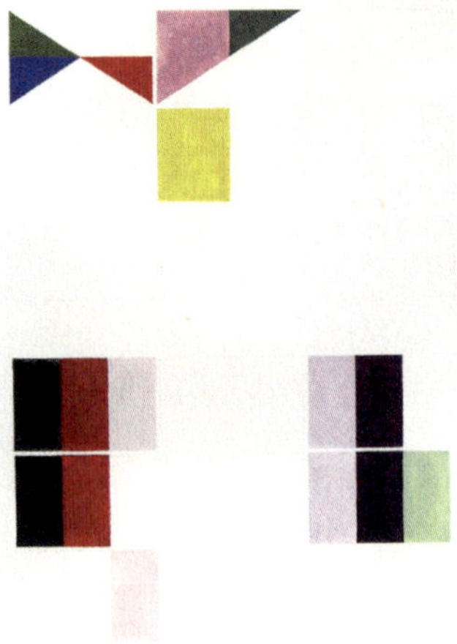

I imagine that, in reality, C hadn't been there for some time. Now, if he were no longer physically present, the garden continued to exist by force of inertia. Or perhaps both were there, and I was the one who found himself in the season described by Albucius, the Athenian philosopher C had alluded to so many times—the season where sponges break [...] and a timeless residue, an illusion of the mind that, nevertheless, seems like a permanent now. A place that is not dystopic nor utopic. The place where language is reformulated before being said.[44]

It defies description.

44 Quignard, 57.

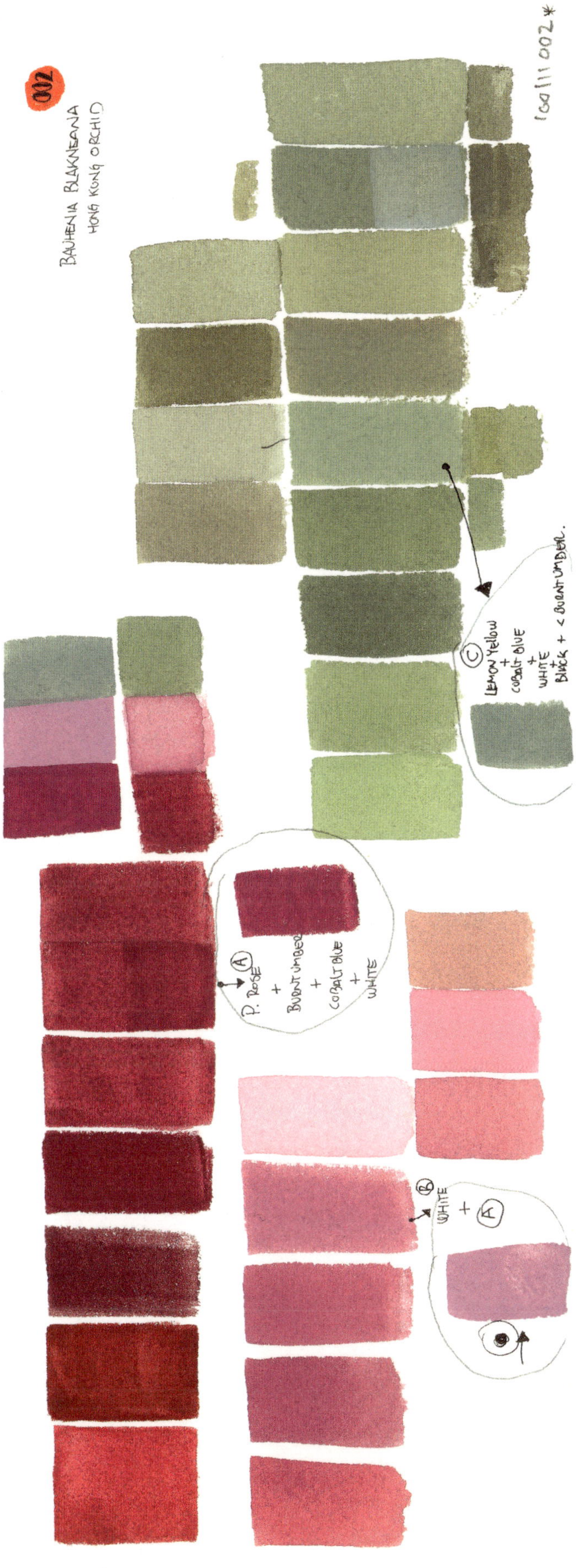
002
BAUHENIA BLAKNEANA
HONG KONG ORCHID
100|11 002*
(C) LEMON YELLOW + COBALT BLUE + WHITE + BLACK + < BURNT UMBER.
P. ROSE (A) + BURNT UMBER + COBALT BLUE + WHITE
(B) WHITE + (A)

005

COPROSMA REPENS
MARBLE QUEEN

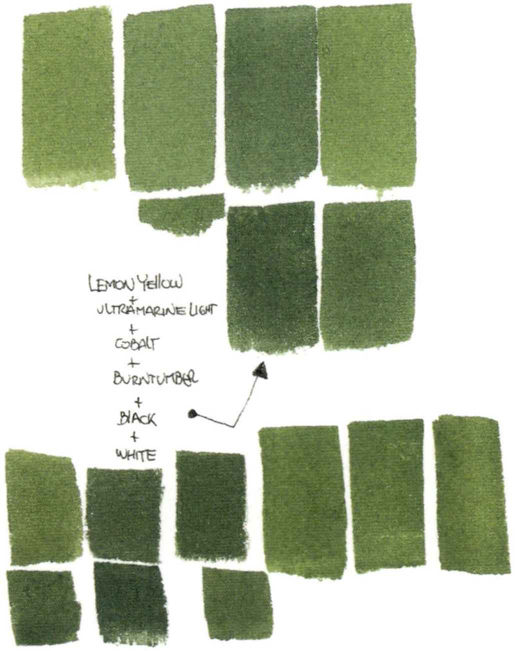

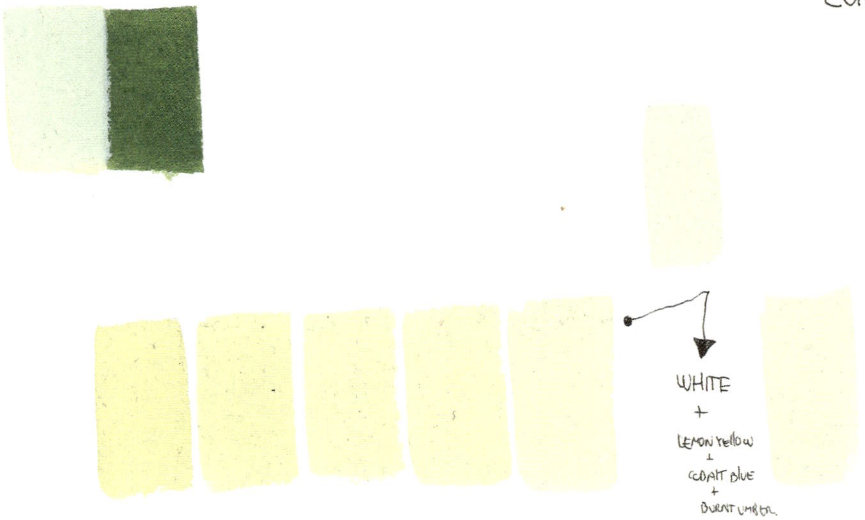

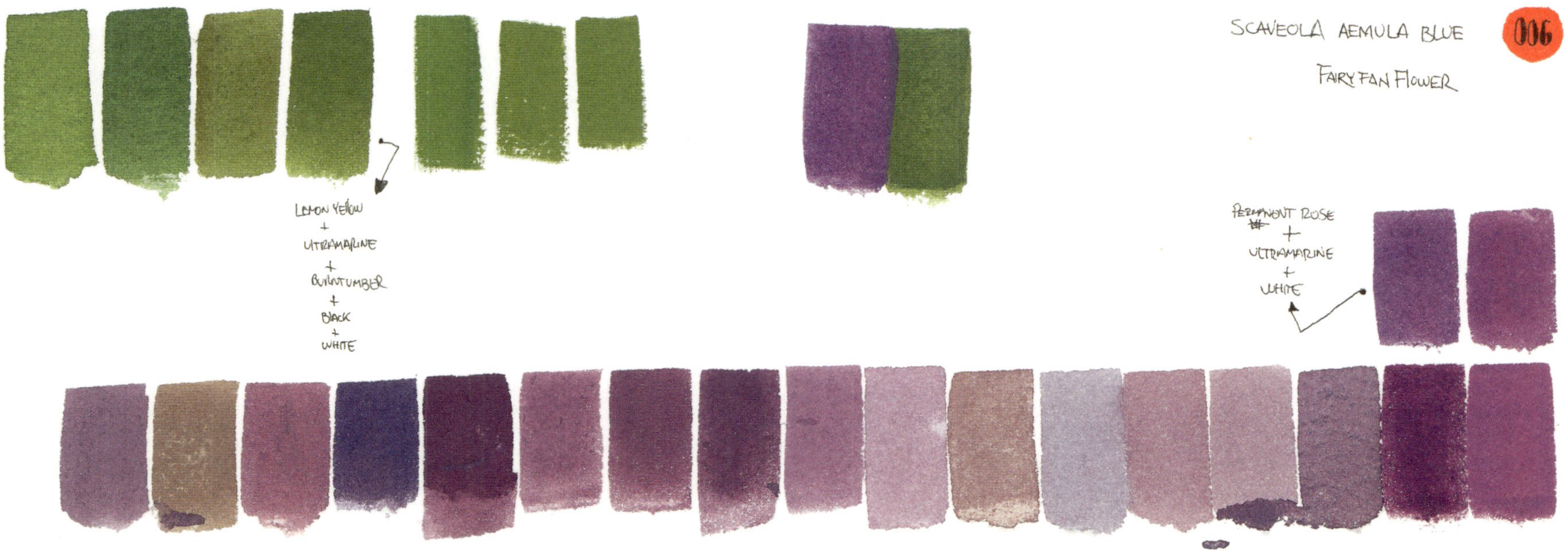
006
SCAVEOLA AEMULA BLUE
FAIRY FAN FLOWER
PERMANENT ROSE + ULTRAMARINE + WHITE
LEMON YELLOW + ULTRAMARINE + BURNT UMBER + BLACK + WHITE

007

LIMONIUM PEREZII

SEA LAVANDER

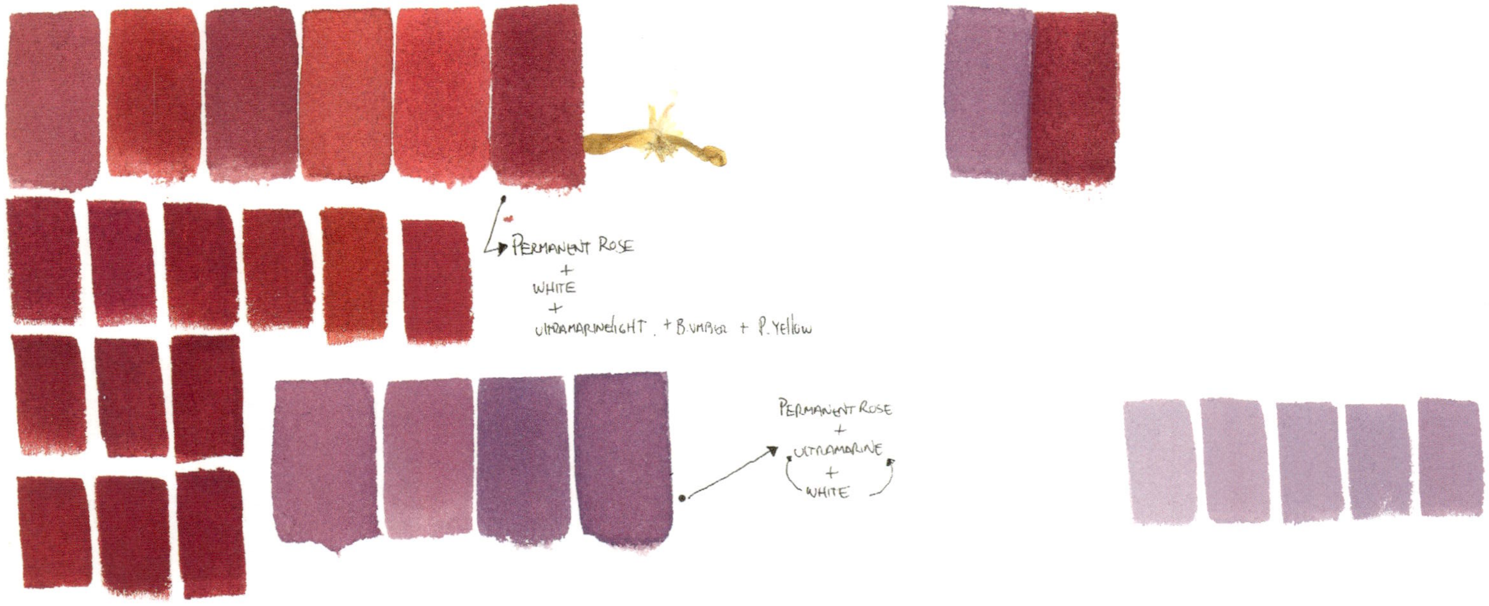

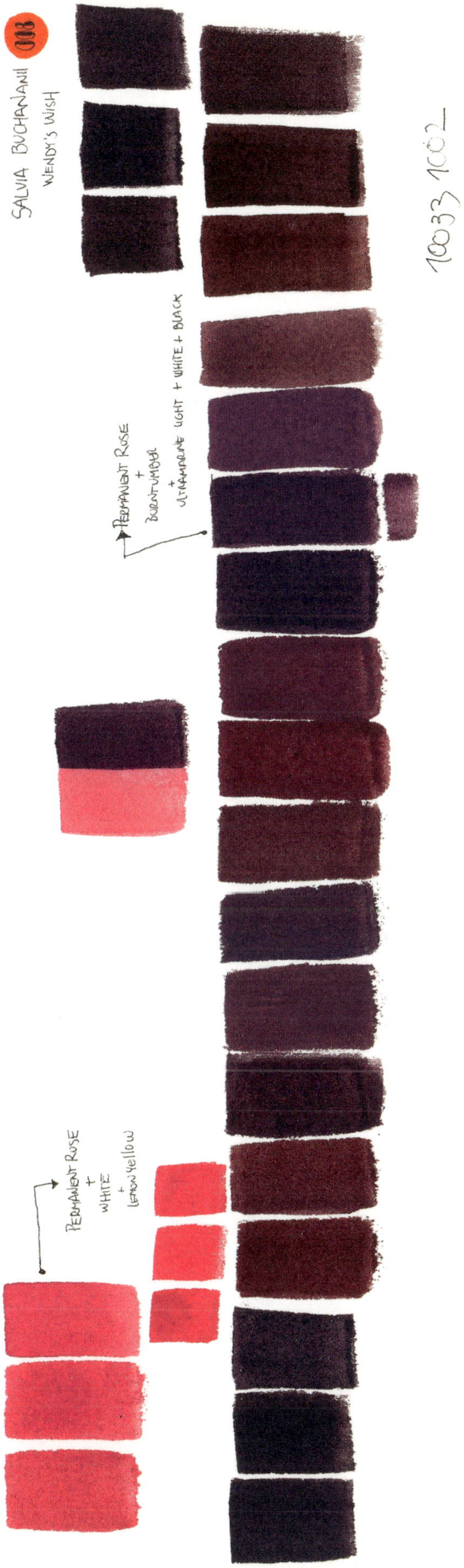
008
SALVIA BUCHANANII
WENDY'S WISH
PERMANENT ROSE + BURNT UMBER + ULTRAMARINE LIGHT + WHITE + BLACK
PERMANENT ROSE + WHITE + LEMON YELLOW

009
SCAVEOLA ALBIDA WHITE
WHIRLWIND WHITE
LEMON YELLOW + WHITE + BURNT UMBER + ULTRAMARINE
ULTRAMARINE + LEMON YELLOW + BURNT UMBER + BLACK + WHITE
WHITE + COBALT BLUE + PERMANENT ROSE

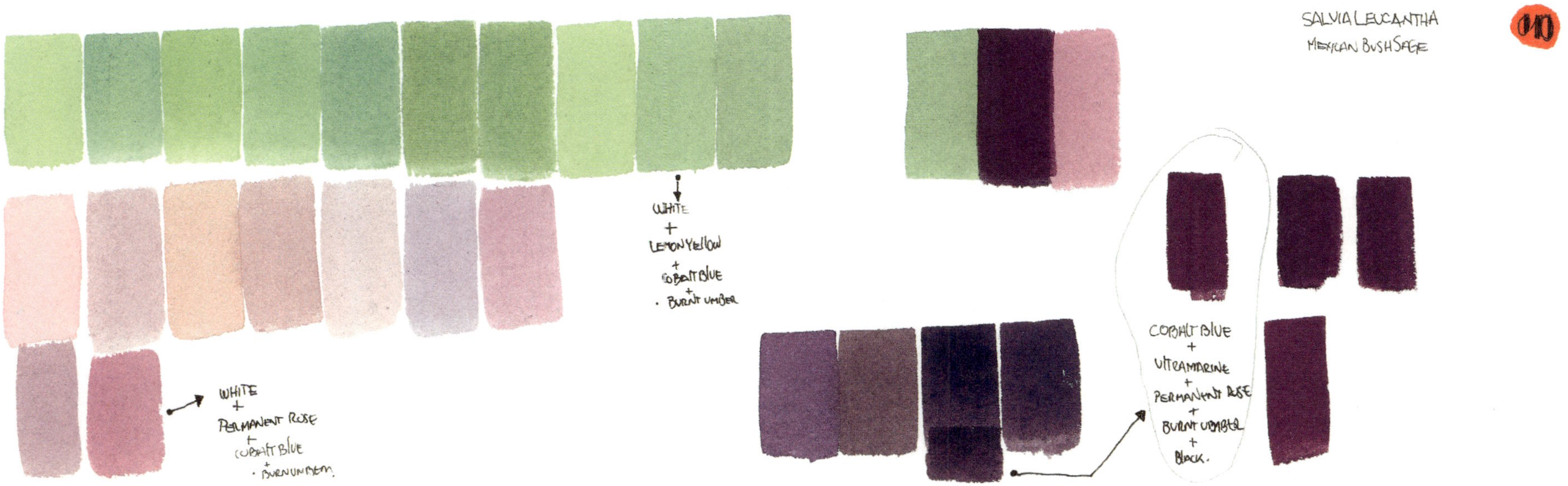
010
SALVIA LEUCANTHA
MEXICAN BUSH SAGE
WHITE + LEMON YELLOW + COBALT BLUE + BURNT UMBER
WHITE + PERMANENT ROSE + COBALT BLUE
COBALT BLUE + ULTRAMARINE + PERMANENT ROSE + BURNT UMBER + BLACK.

011

VITEX TRIFOLIA PURPUREA

ARABIAN LILAC

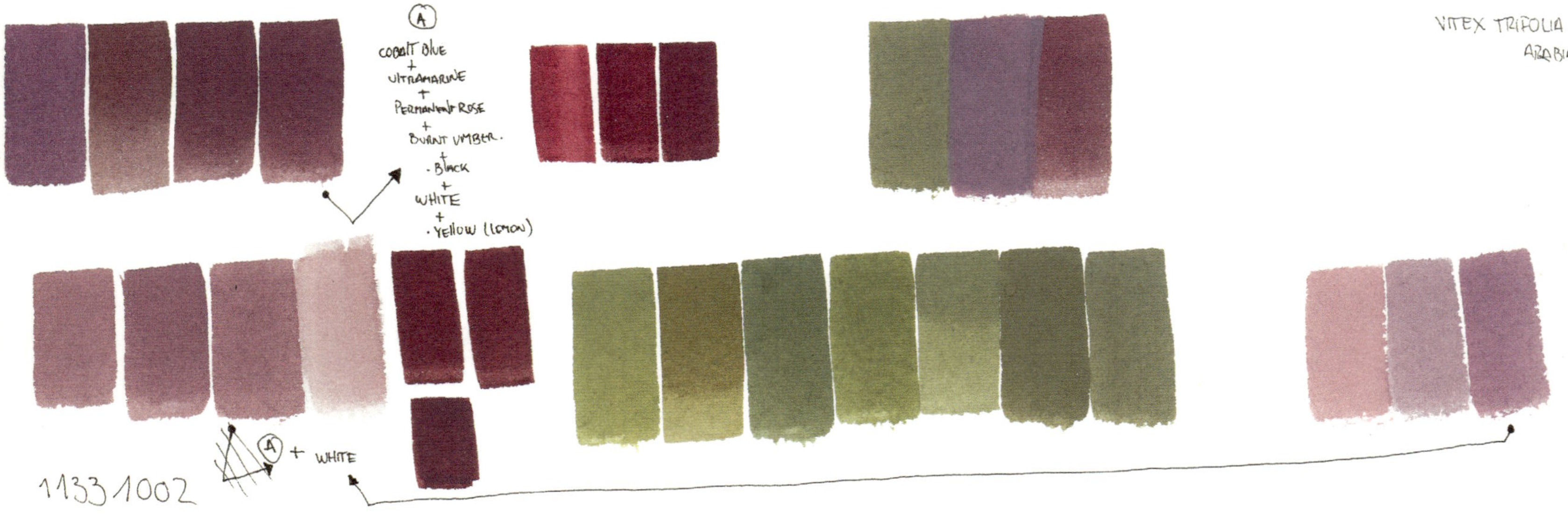

LEONOTIS LEONURUS 012

LION'S TAIL

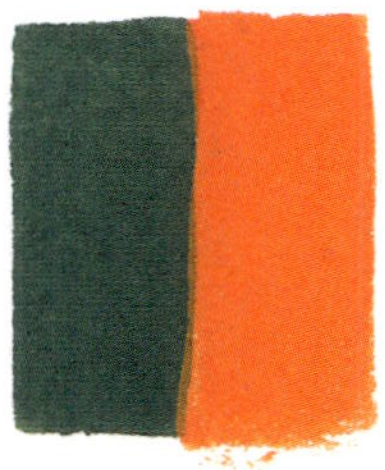

015 DIPLADENIA MANDEVILLA

REDRIDDING HOOD

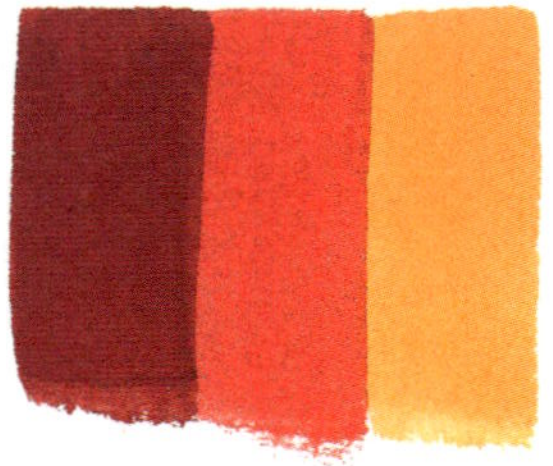

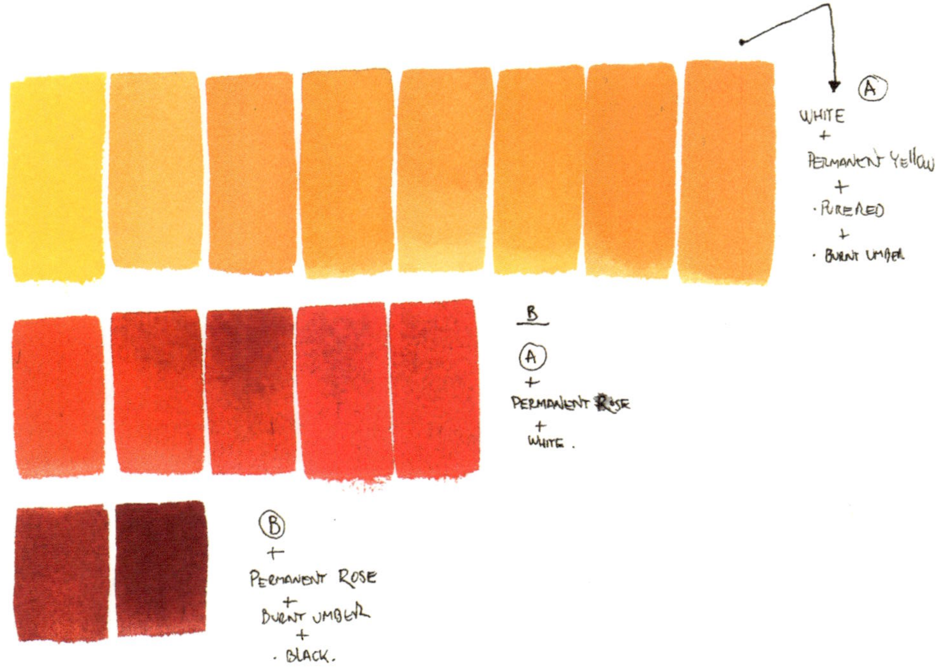

100331002

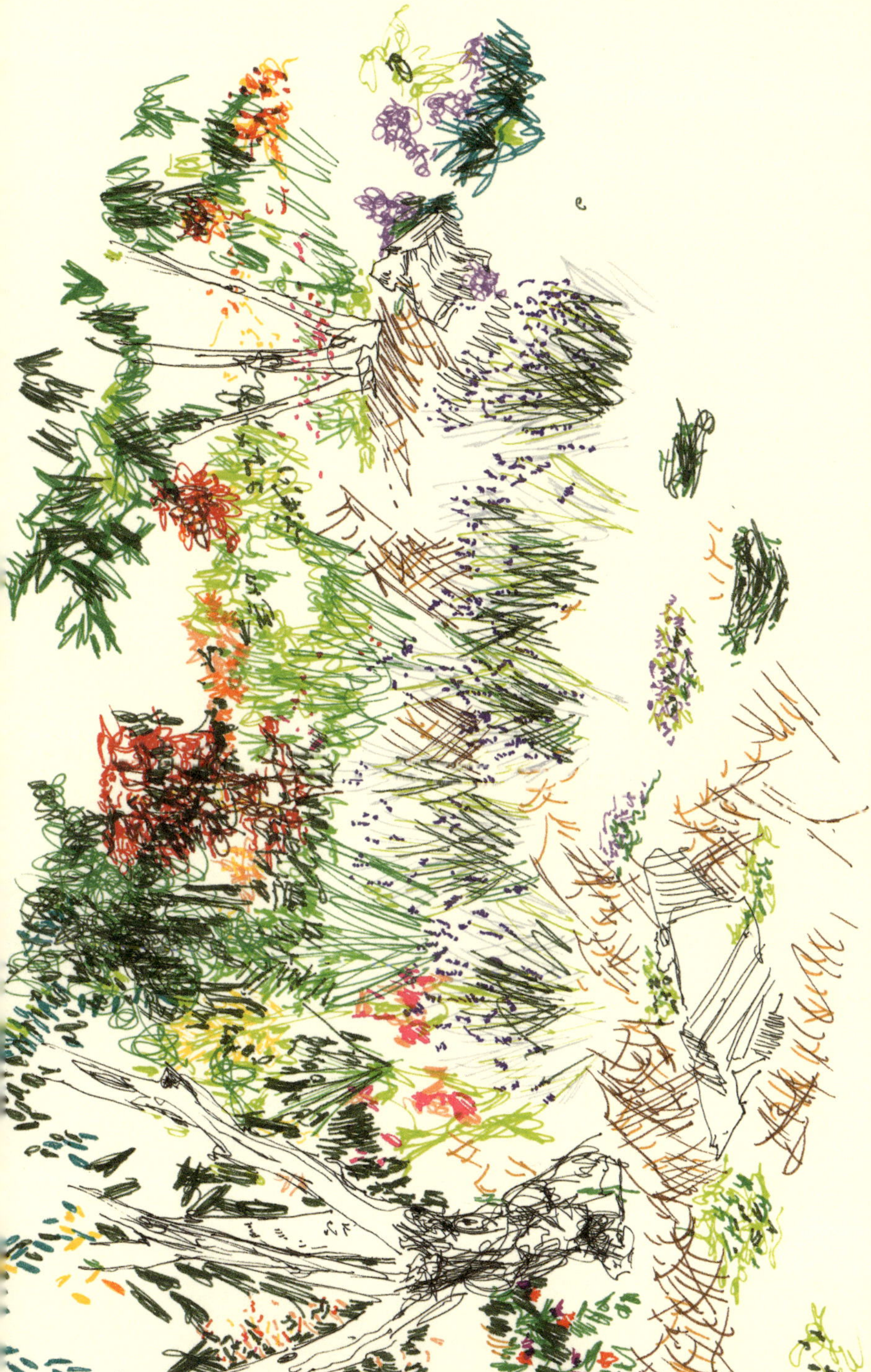

Color sketch of the *haudenschild*Garage garden (2017)

Boceto de color del jardín del *haudenschild*Garage (2017)

VARIEGATED DURANTA 016
SKYFLOWER GOLDEN EDGE.

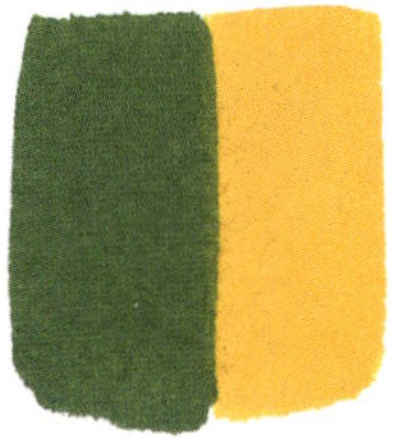

A
WHITE
+
LEMON YELLOW
+
PERMANENT YELLOW
+
. BURNT UMBER.

A
+
ULTRAMARINE
+
. BURNT UMBER.

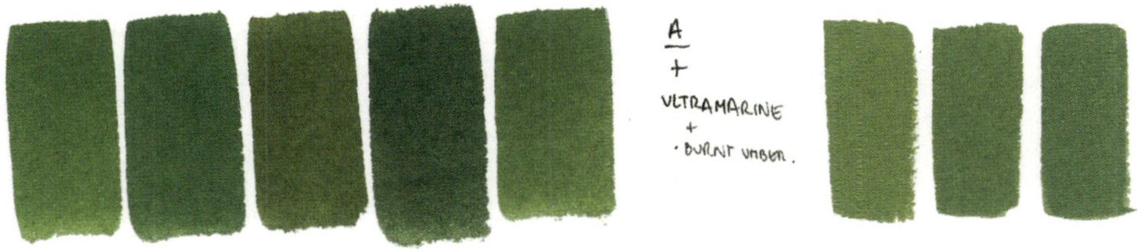

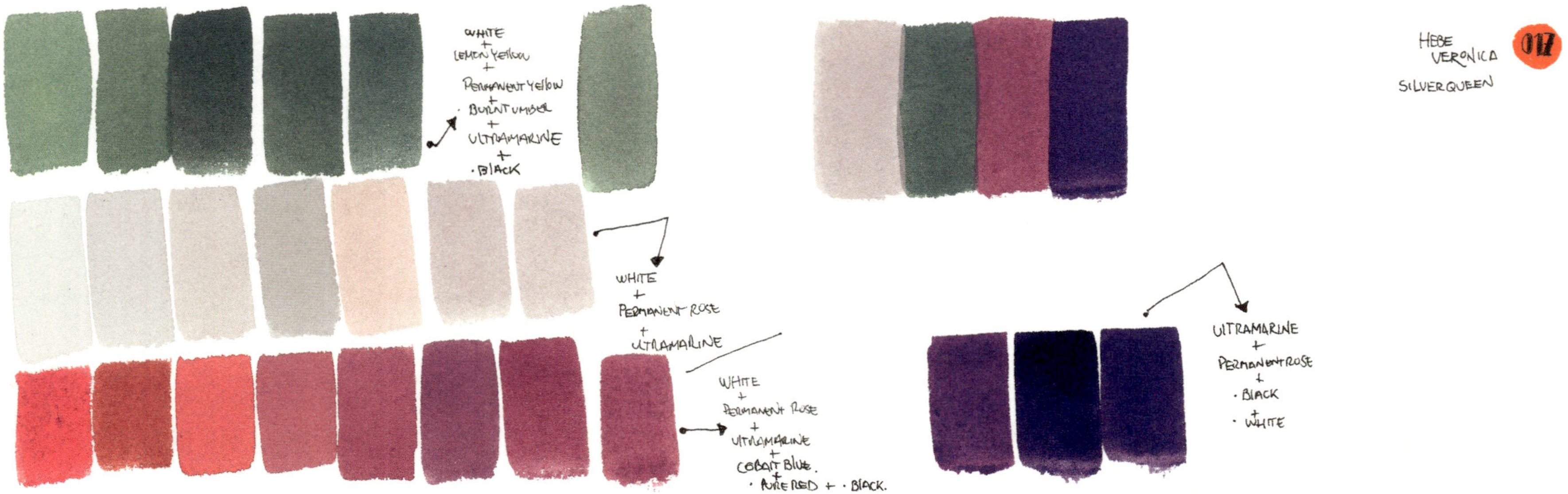
017
HEBE VERONICA
SILVER QUEEN
WHITE + LEMON YELLOW + PERMANENT YELLOW + · BURNT UMBER + ULTRAMARINE + · BLACK
WHITE + PERMANENT ROSE + ULTRAMARINE
WHITE + PERMANENT ROSE + ULTRAMARINE + COBALT BLUE. + · PURE RED + · BLACK.
ULTRAMARINE + PERMANENT ROSE + · BLACK + · WHITE

018

LANTANA CAMARA

GOLDMOUND

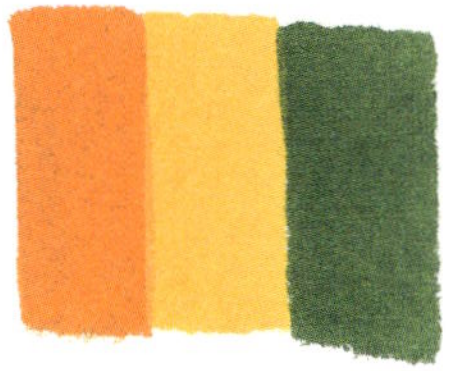

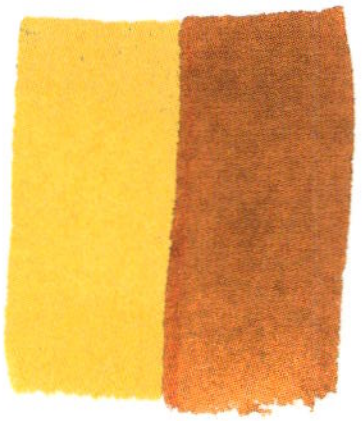

LEMON YELLOW
+
PERMANENT YELLOW
+
· BURNT UMBER
+
· WHITE

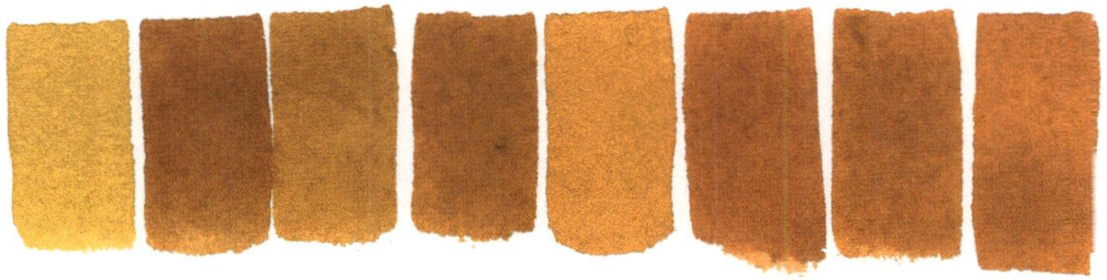

PERMANENT YELLOW
+
LEMON YELLOW
+
PURE RED
+
BURNT UMBER
+
· WHITE.

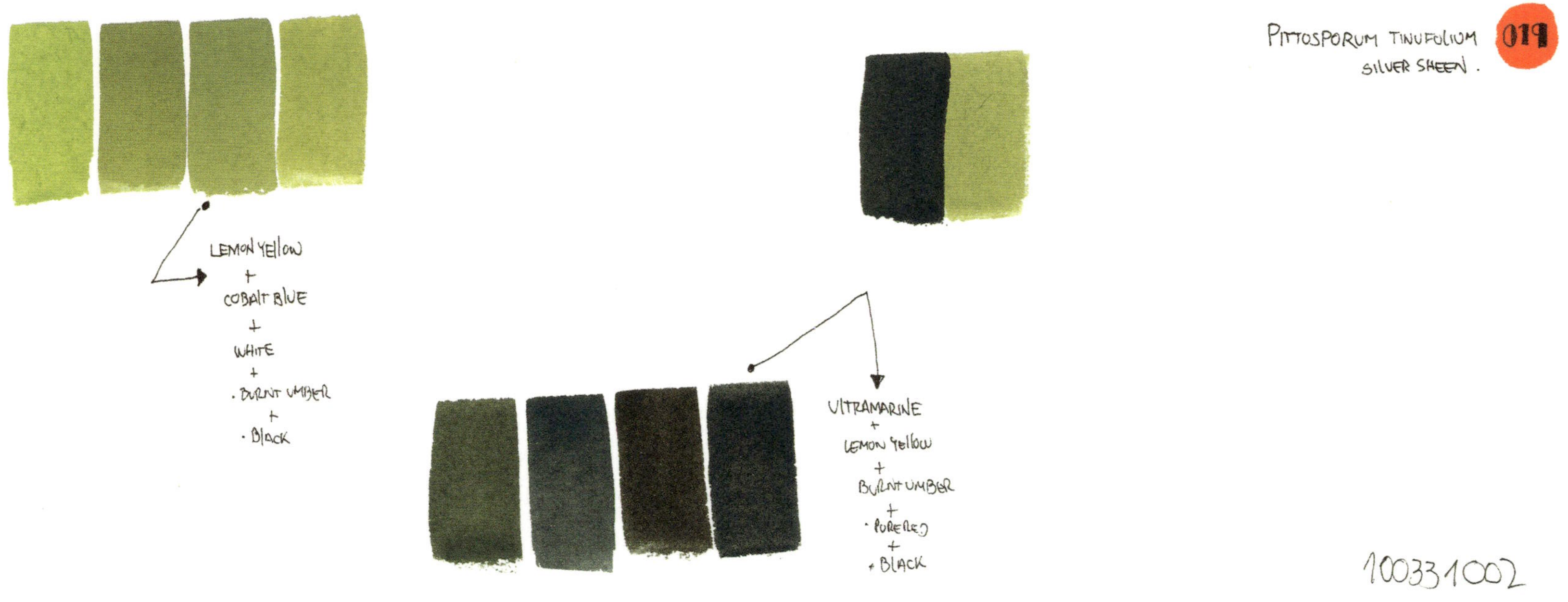
019
PITTOSPORUM TINUFOLIUM
SILVER SHEEN .
LEMON YELLOW
+
COBALT BLUE
+
WHITE
+
· BURNT UMBER
+
· BLACK
ULTRAMARINE
+
LEMON YELLOW
+
BURNT UMBER
+
· PURE RED
+
· BLACK
100331002

020 Coprosoma Repens

Mirror Plant

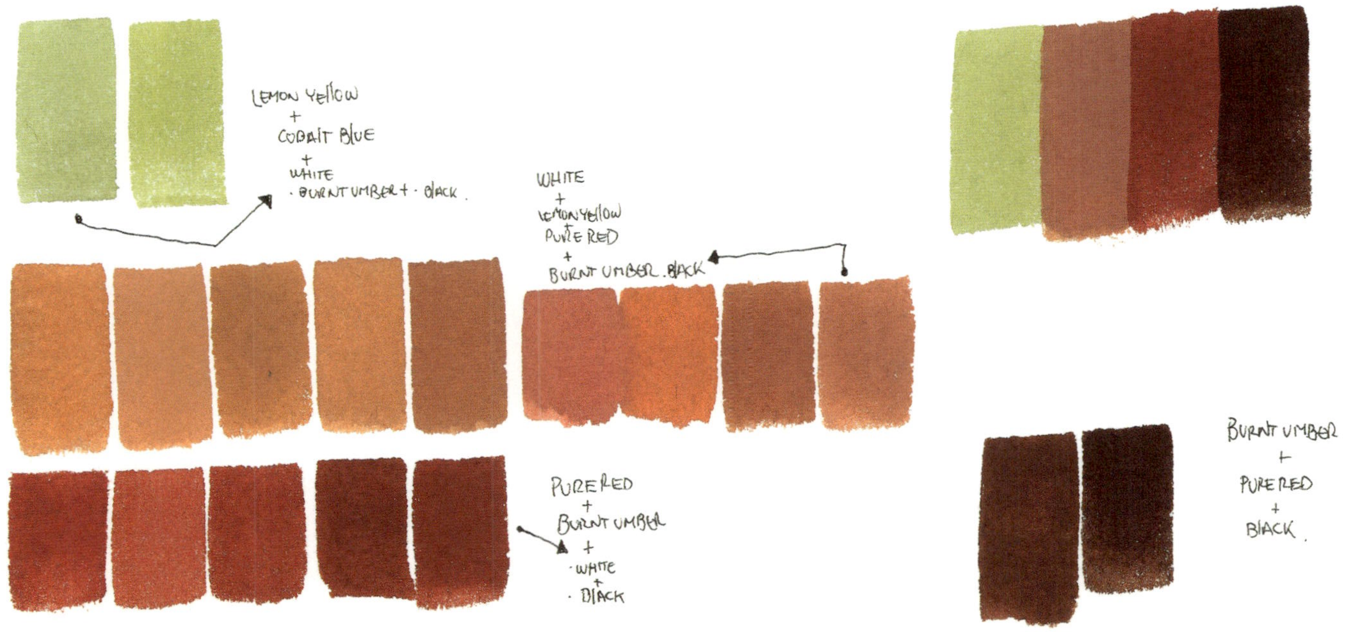

021

BAUHINIA GALPINI
RED ORCHID BUSH

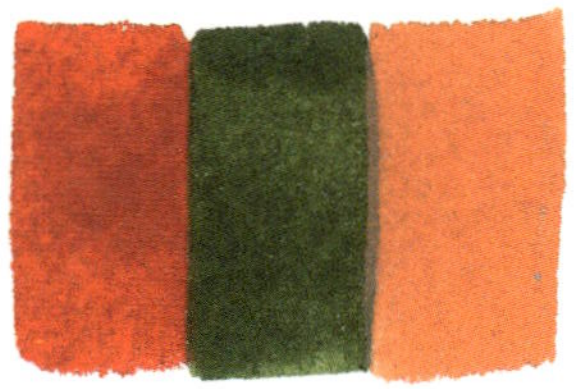

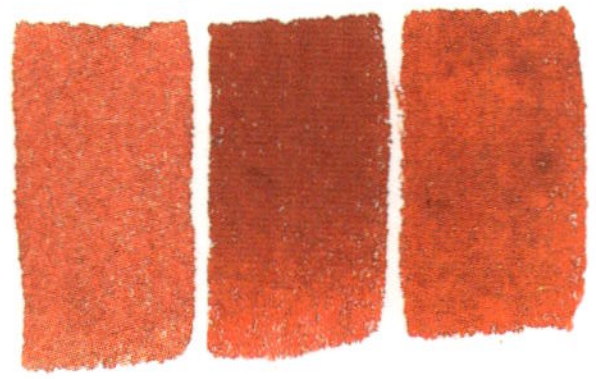

PURE RED
+
PERMANENT YELLOW
+
· WHITE
+
· BURNT UMBER.

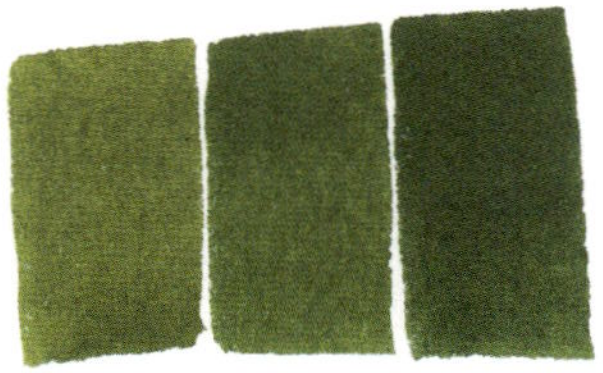

WHITE
+
PURE RED
+
PERMANENT YELLOW
+
· BURNT UMBER.

022

Breynia Distichia

Dwarf Snow Bush

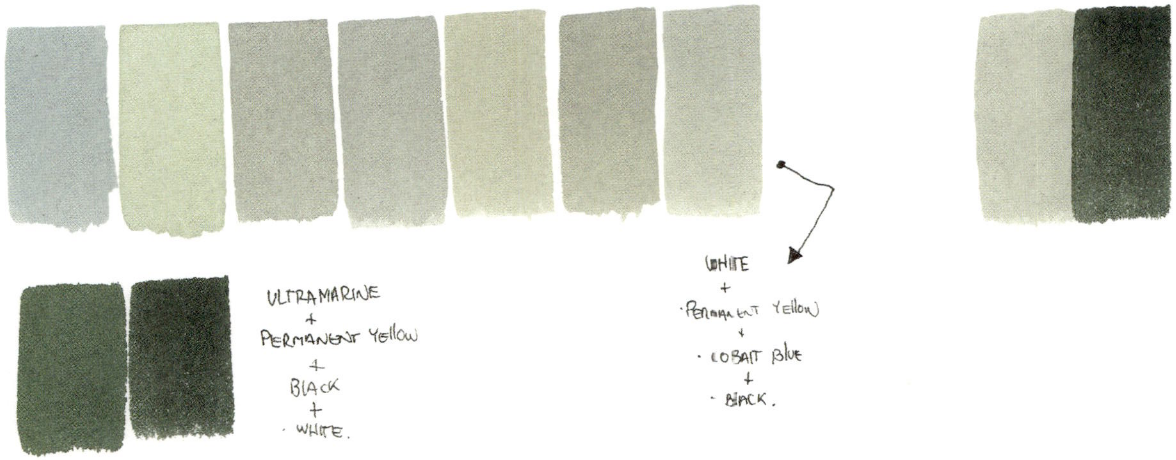

023

Caesalpinia Gilliesii
Desert Bird of Paradise.

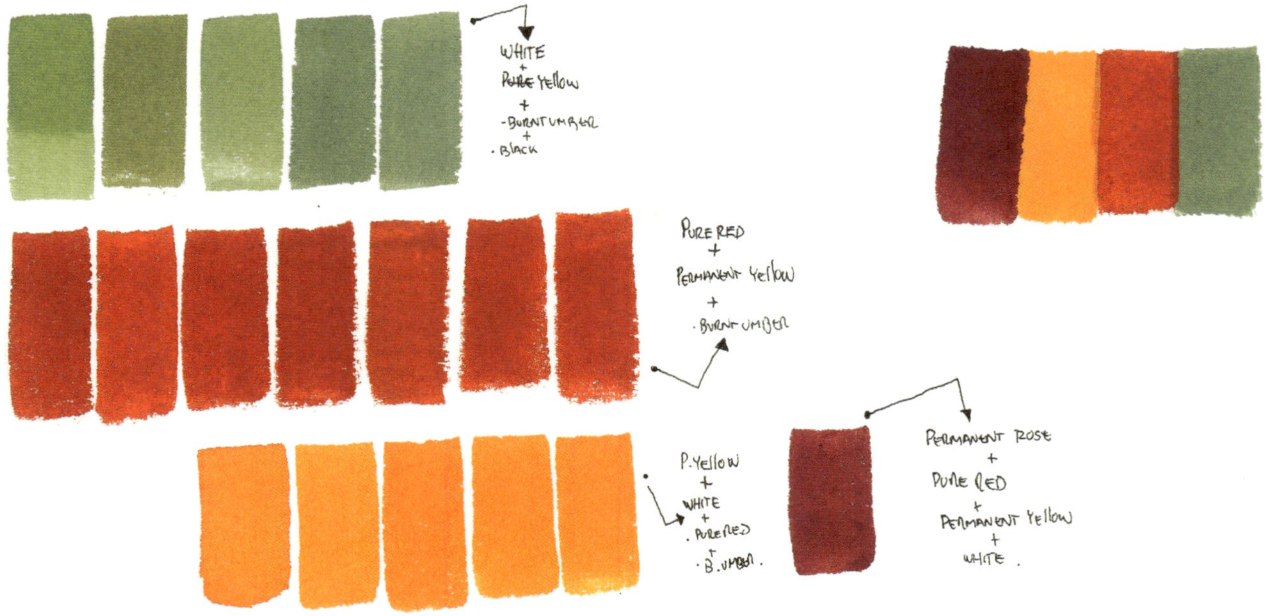

LAVENDULA DENTATA 024

FRENCH LAVANDER.

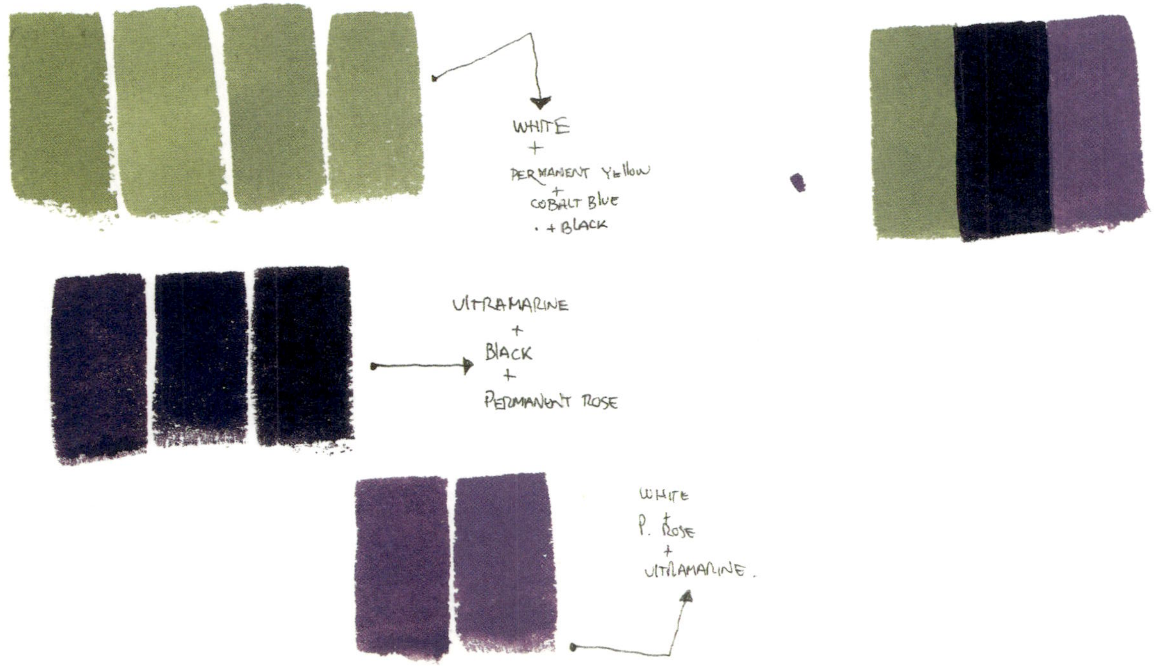

SALVIA MICROPHYLLA 025

LIPSTICK / HOTLIPS.

WHITE
+
· COBALT BLUE

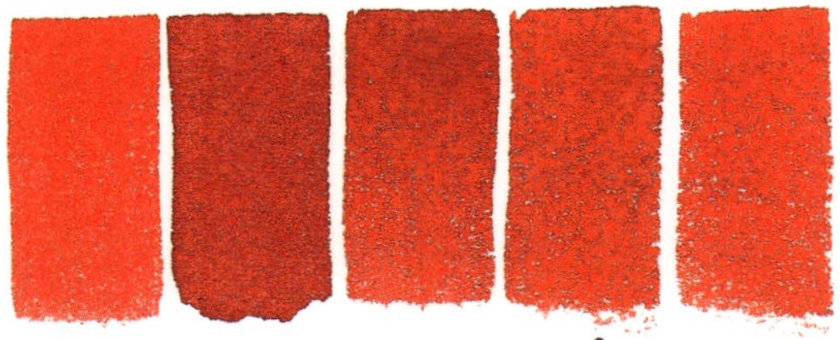

PURE RED
+
· BURNT UMBER
+
· PERMANENT YELLOW

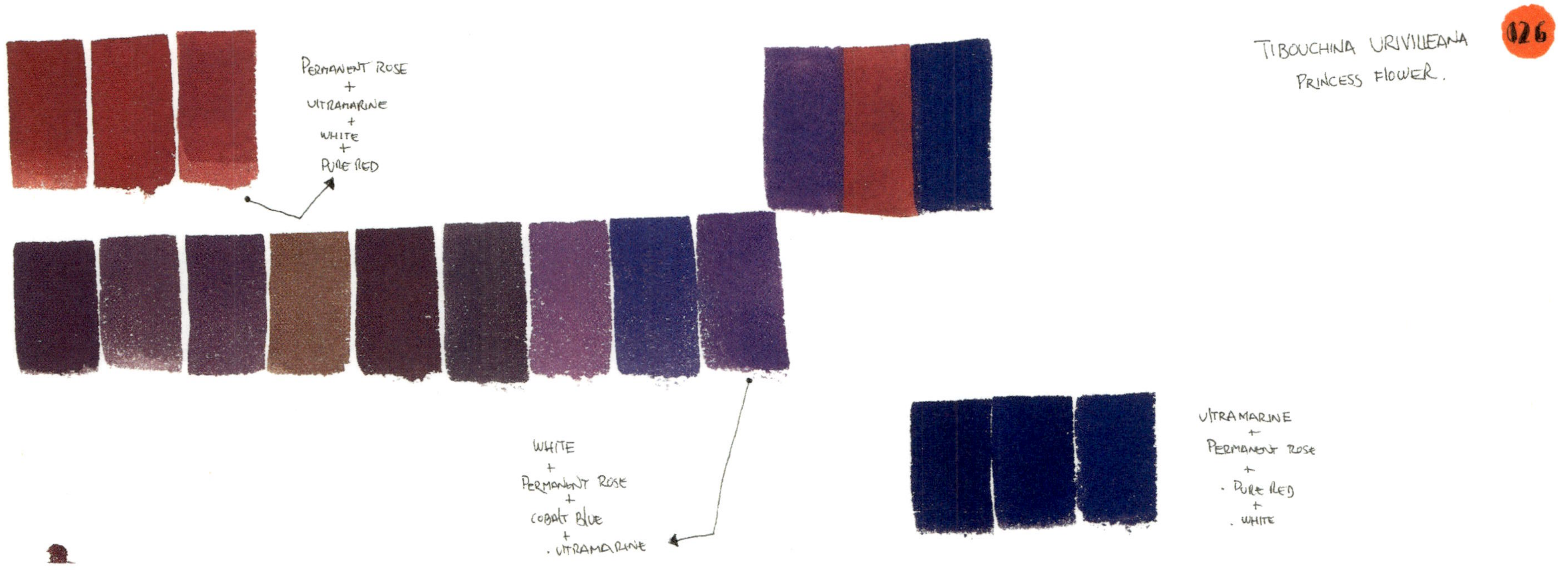
026
TIBOUCHINA URVILLEANA
PRINCESS FLOWER.
PERMANENT ROSE + ULTRAMARINE + WHITE + PURE RED
WHITE + PERMANENT ROSE + COBALT BLUE + . ULTRAMARINE
ULTRAMARINE + PERMANENT ROSE + . PURE RED + . WHITE

029

PODACARPUS GRACILOR

FERN PINE.

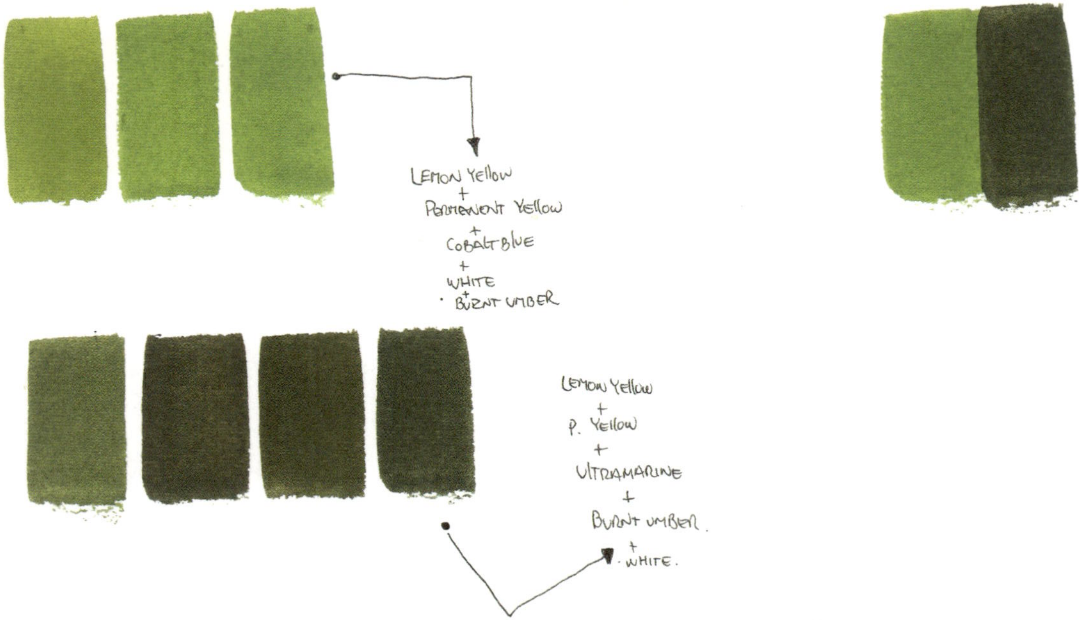

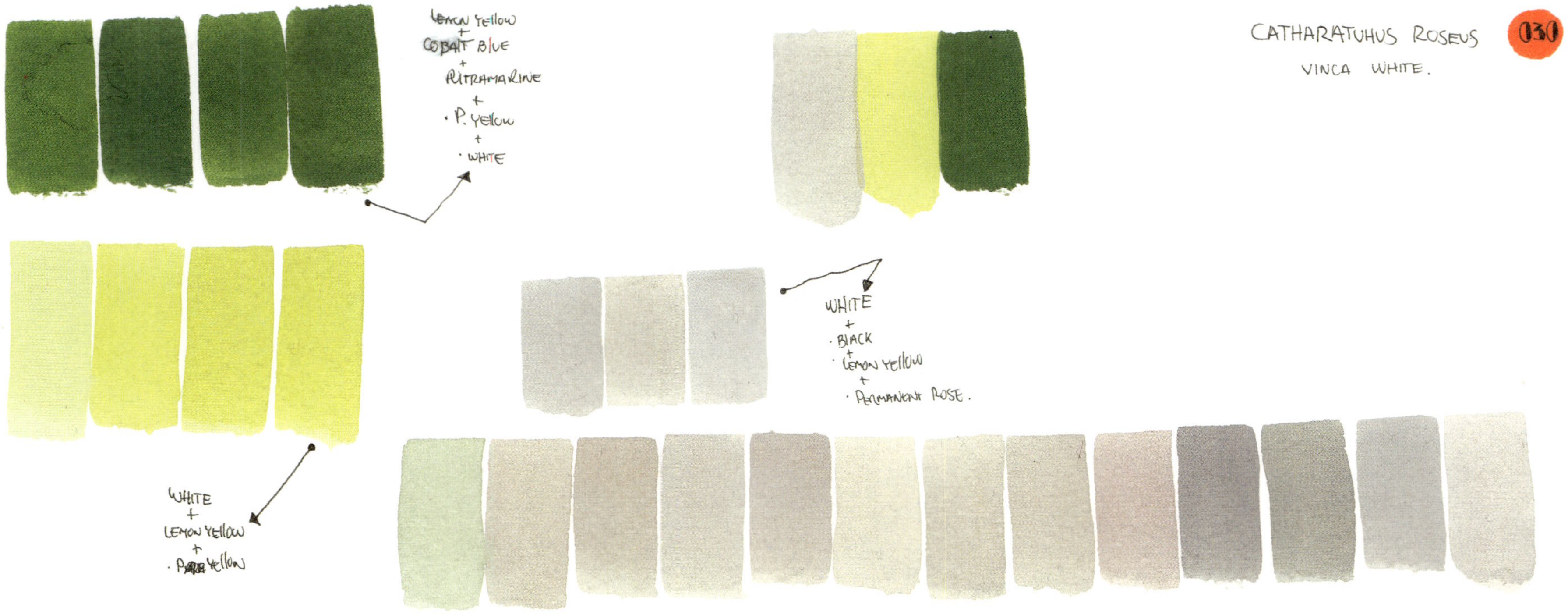
030
CATHARATUHUS ROSEUS
VINCA WHITE.
LEMON YELLOW + COBALT BLUE + ULTRAMARINE + P. YELLOW + WHITE
WHITE + BLACK + LEMON YELLOW + PERMANENT ROSE.
WHITE + LEMON YELLOW + P. YELLOW

ANGIO ZANTHOS **031**

KANGAROO PAWS ORANGE.

PURE RED
+
PERMANENT YELLOW
+
BURNT UMBER
+
WHITE

032

ACACIA COGNATA
COUSIN ITT

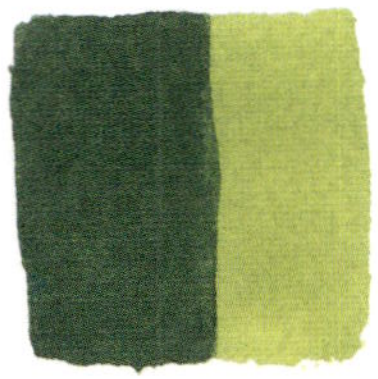

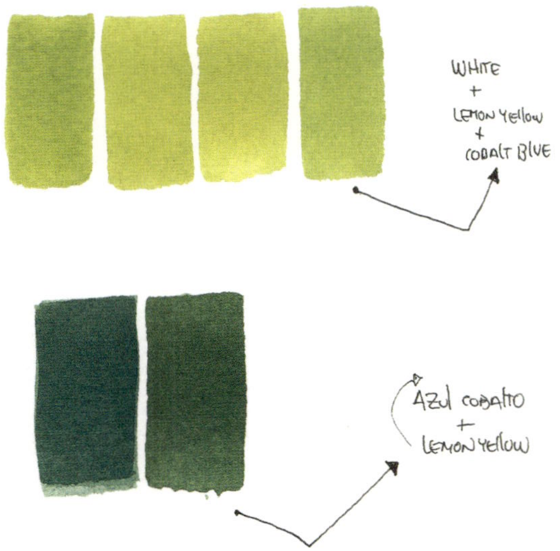

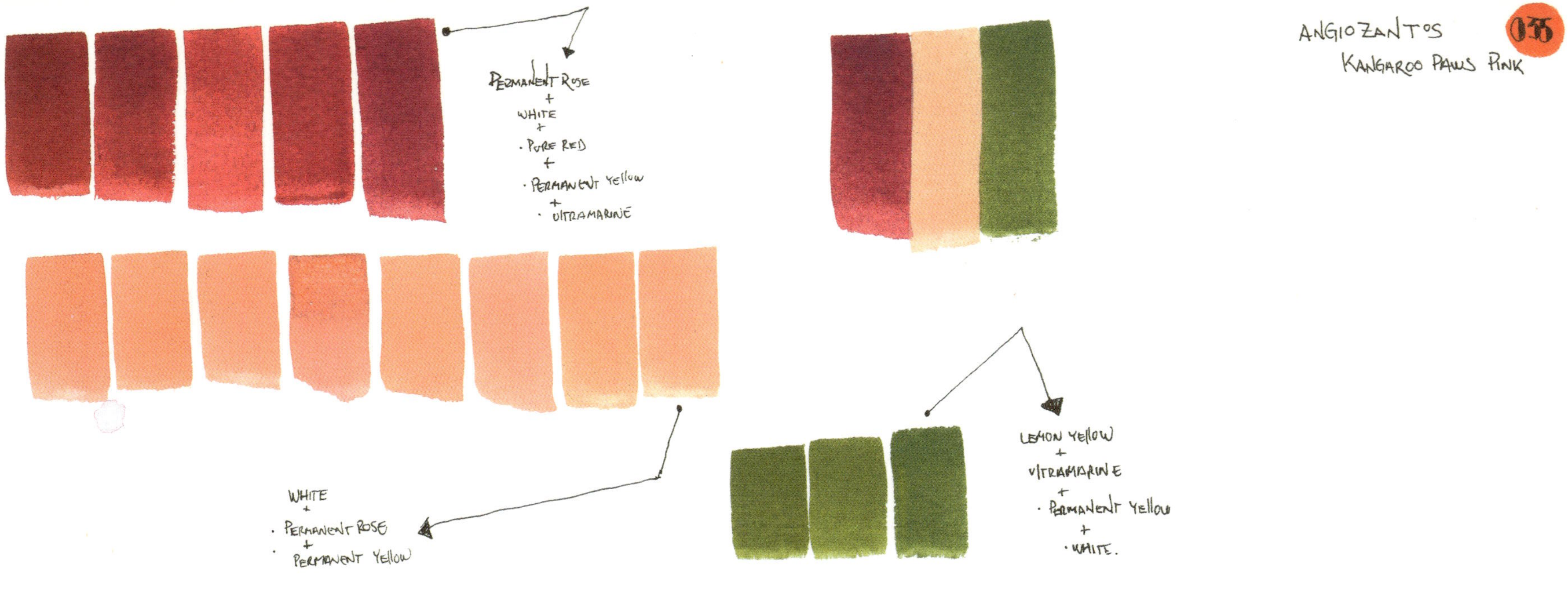
035
Angiozantos
Kangaroo Paws Pink
Permanent Rose + White + · Pure Red + · Permanent Yellow + · Ultramarine
White + · Permanent Rose + · Permanent Yellow
Lemon Yellow + Ultramarine + · Permanent Yellow + · White.

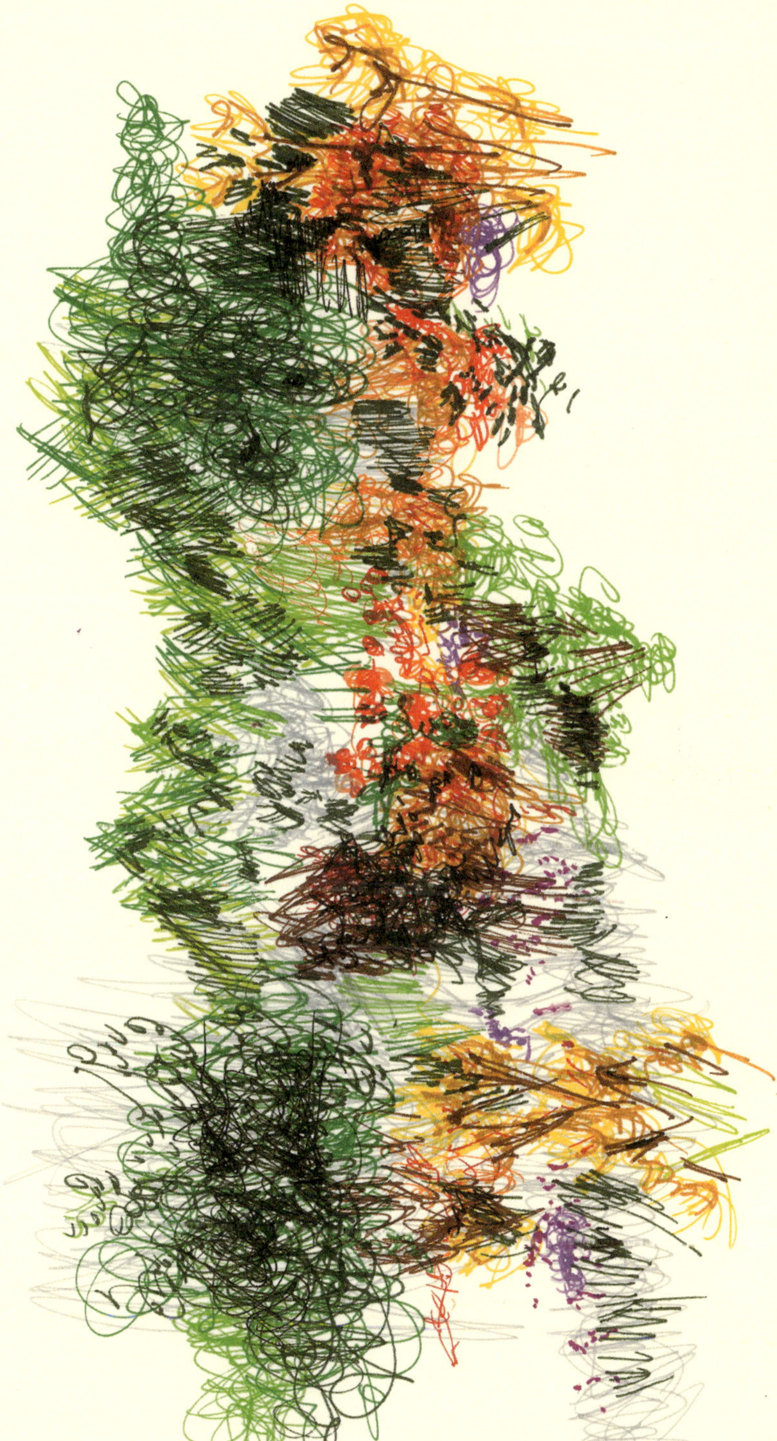

Color sketch of the *haudenschild*Garage garden (2017)

Boceto de color del jardín del *haudenschild*Garage (2017)

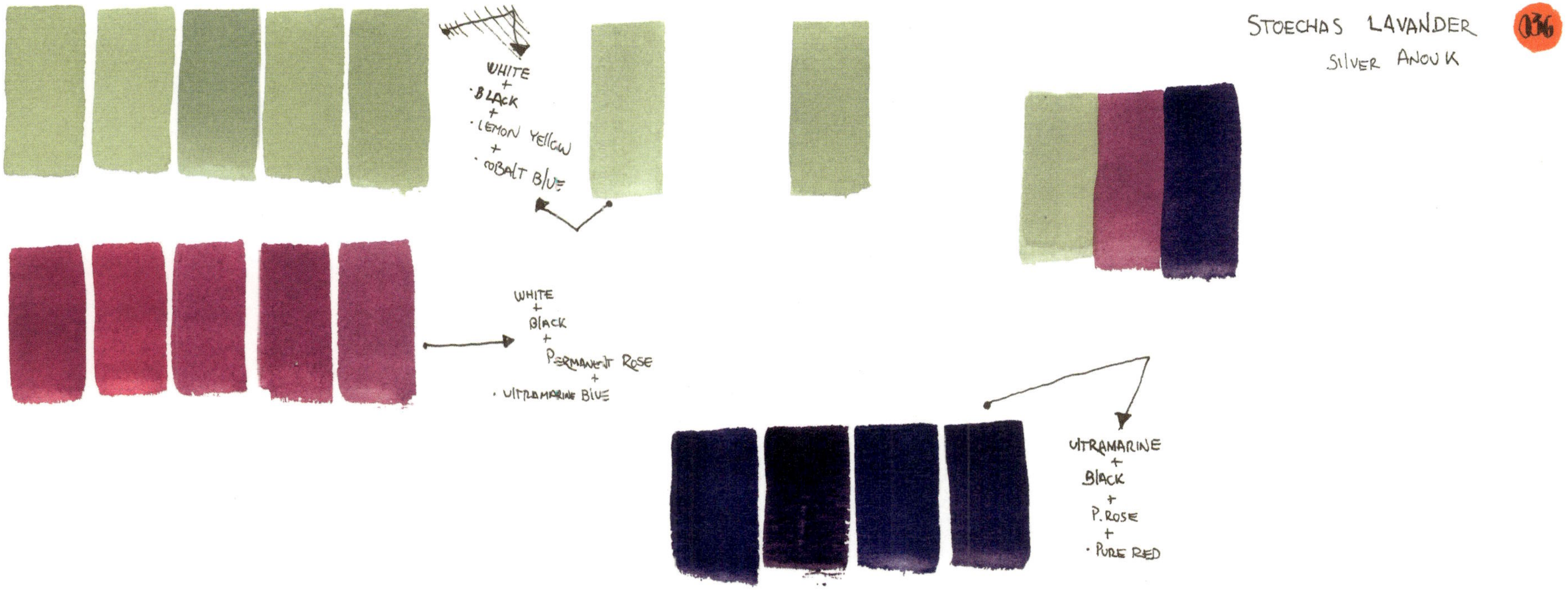
036
STOECHAS LAVANDER
SILVER ANOUK
WHITE + BLACK + LEMON YELLOW + COBALT BLUE
WHITE + BLACK + PERMANENT ROSE + ULTRAMARINE BLUE
ULTRAMARINE + BLACK + P. ROSE + PURE RED

ICEBERG ROSE 037

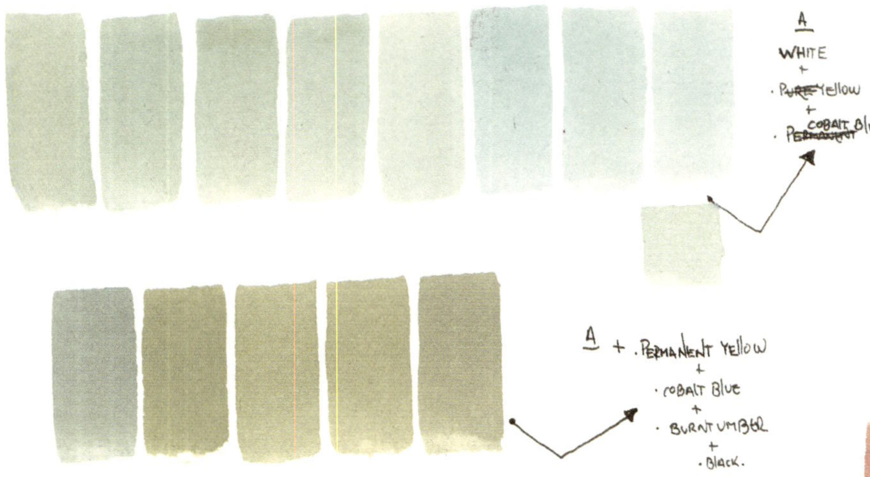

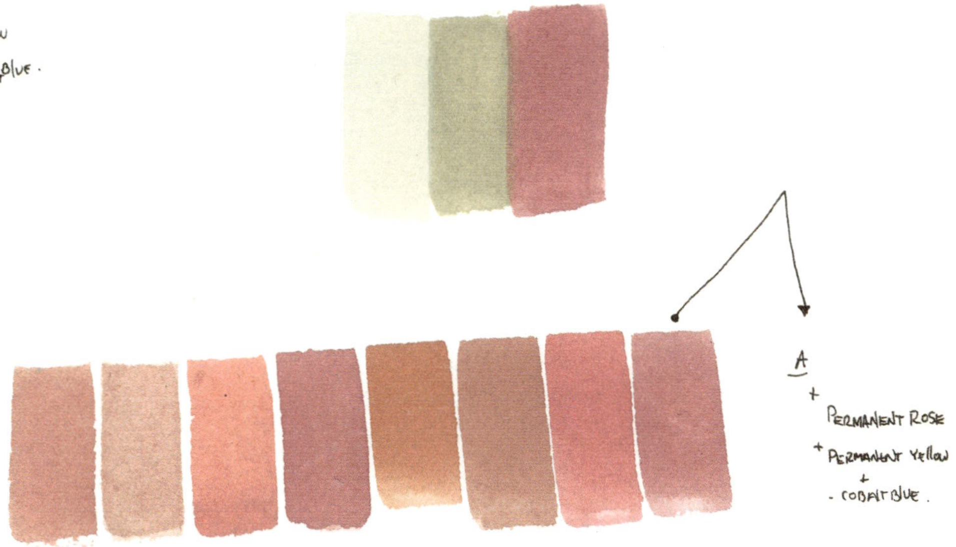

038

FEIJOA SELLOWIANA

PINAPPLE GUAVA

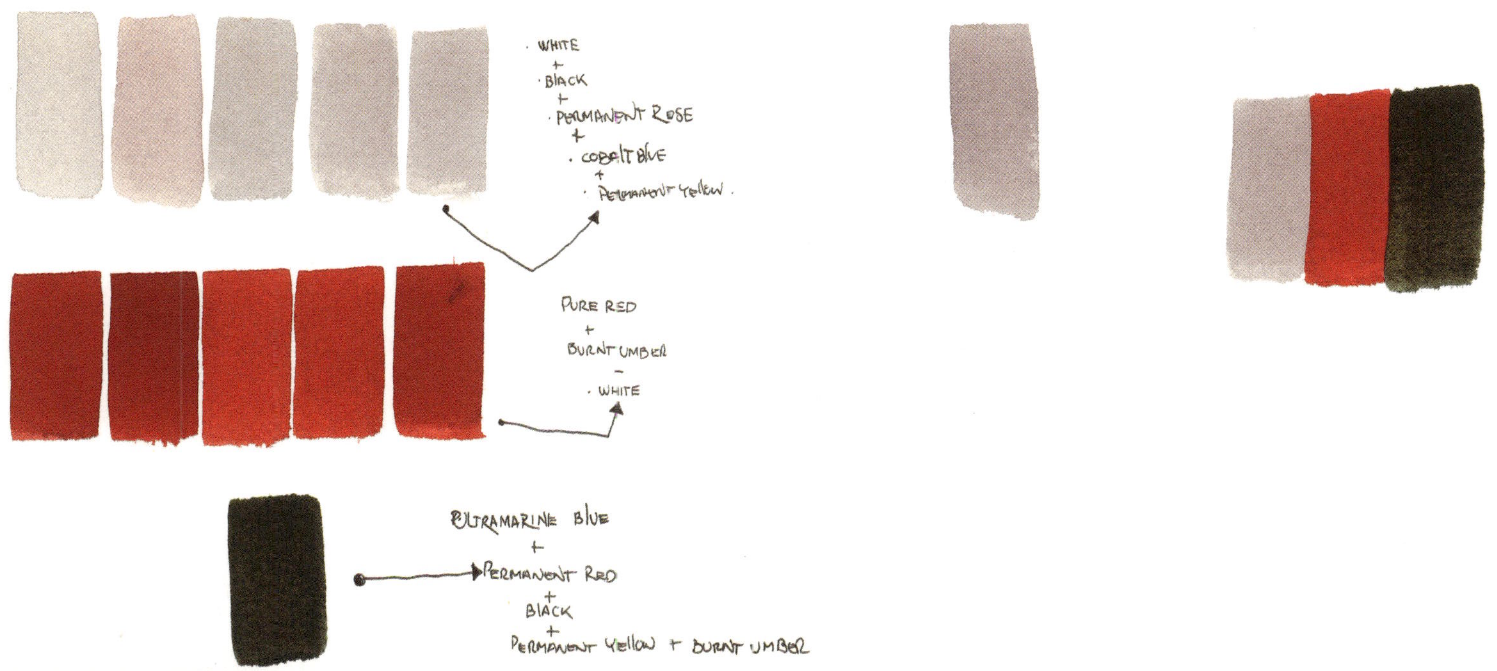

COTINUS COGGYGRIA 039

SMOKE TREE.

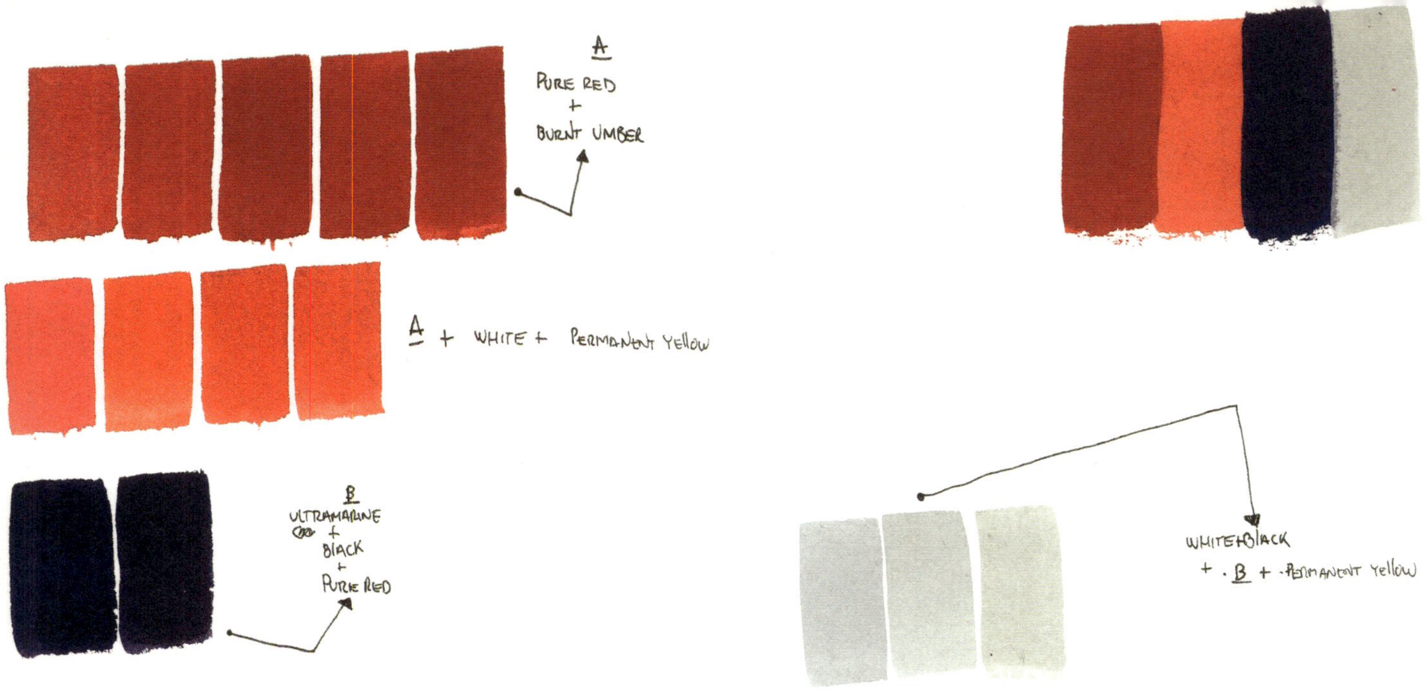

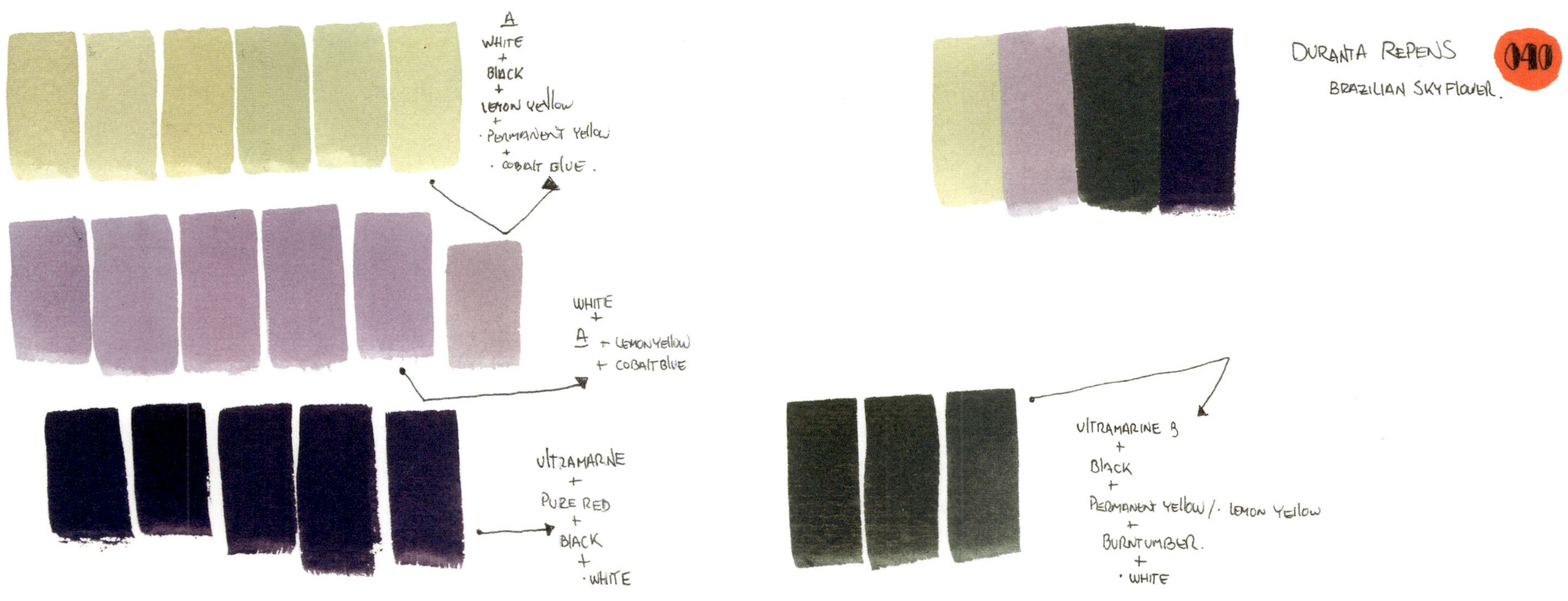
040
DURANTA REPENS
BRAZILIAN SKYFLOWER.
A
WHITE + BLACK + LEMON YELLOW + · PERMANENT YELLOW + · COBALT BLUE.
WHITE + A + LEMON YELLOW + COBALT BLUE
ULTRAMARNE + PURE RED + BLACK + · WHITE
ULTRAMARINE B + BLACK + PERMANENT YELLOW / · LEMON YELLOW + BURNTUMBER. + · WHITE

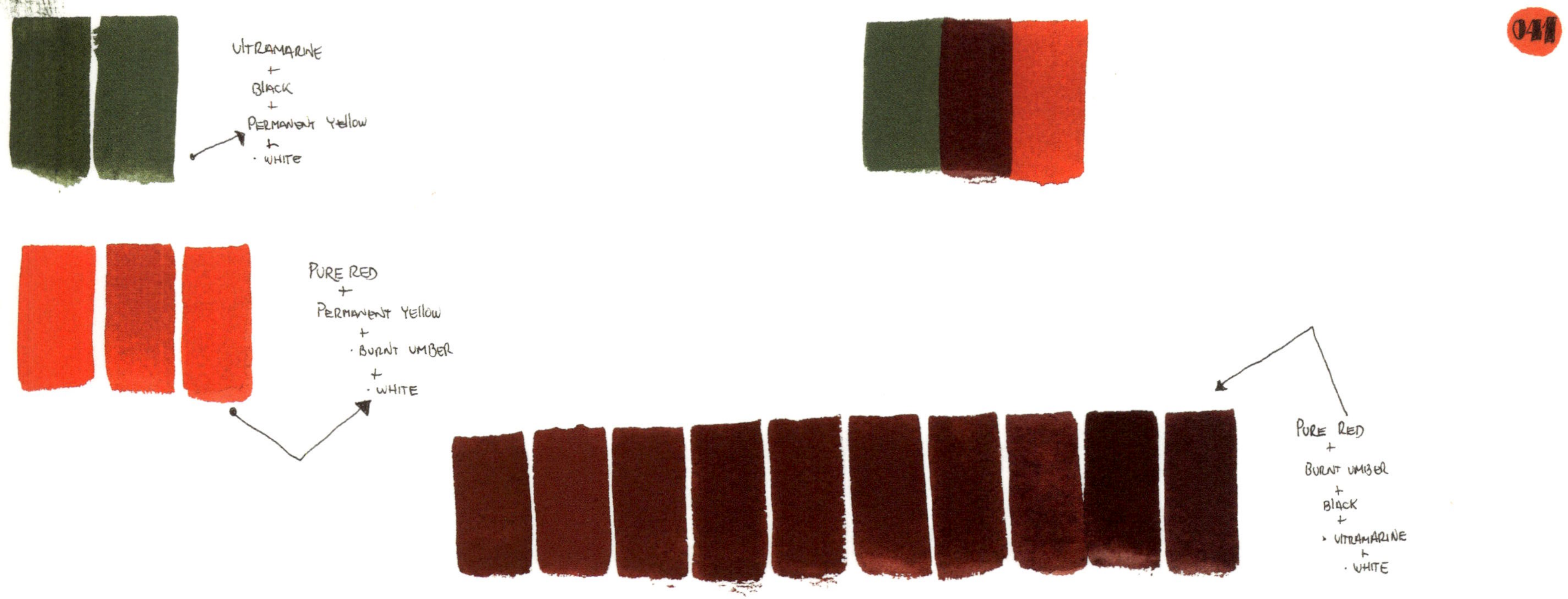
041
ULTRAMARINE + BLACK + PERMANENT YELLOW + · WHITE
PURE RED + PERMANENT YELLOW + · BURNT UMBER + · WHITE
PURE RED + BURNT UMBER + BLACK + · ULTRAMARINE + · WHITE

PLATANUS RACEMOSA 042

CALIFORNIA SYCAMORE.

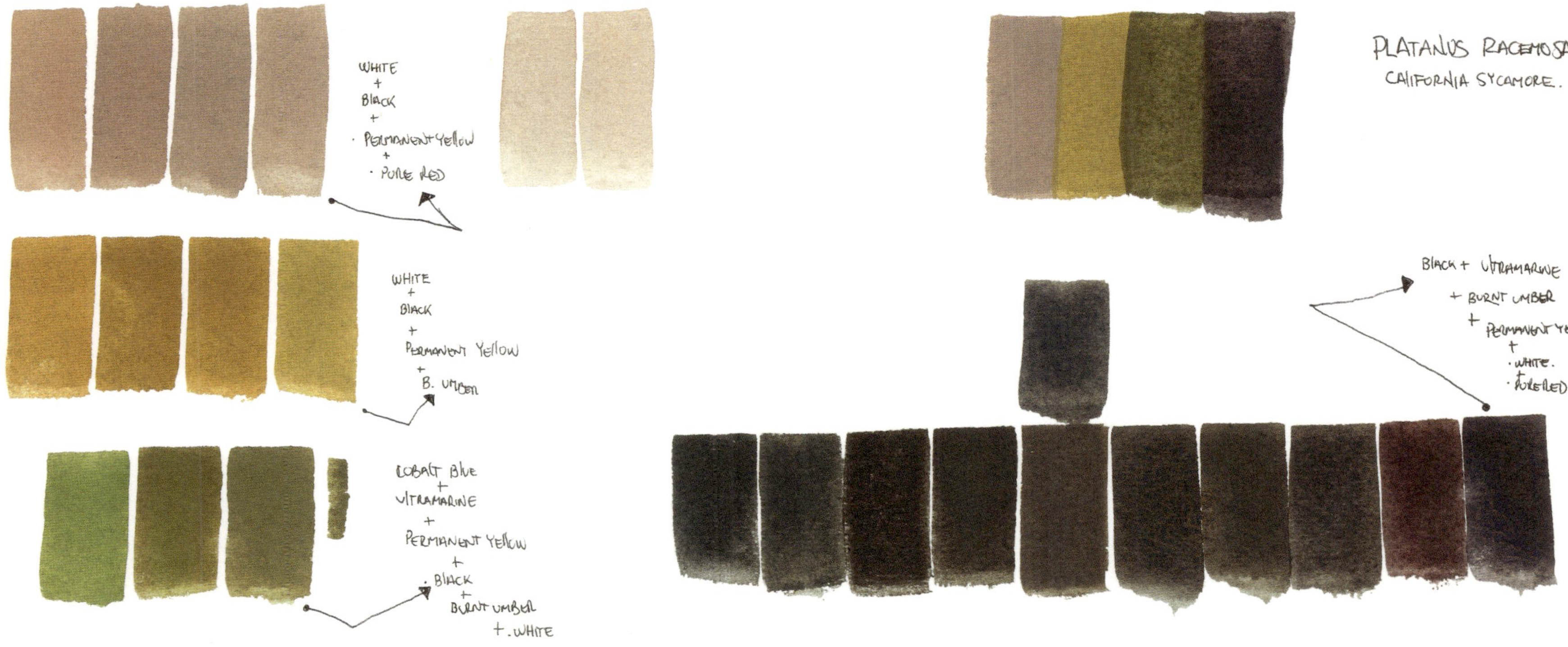

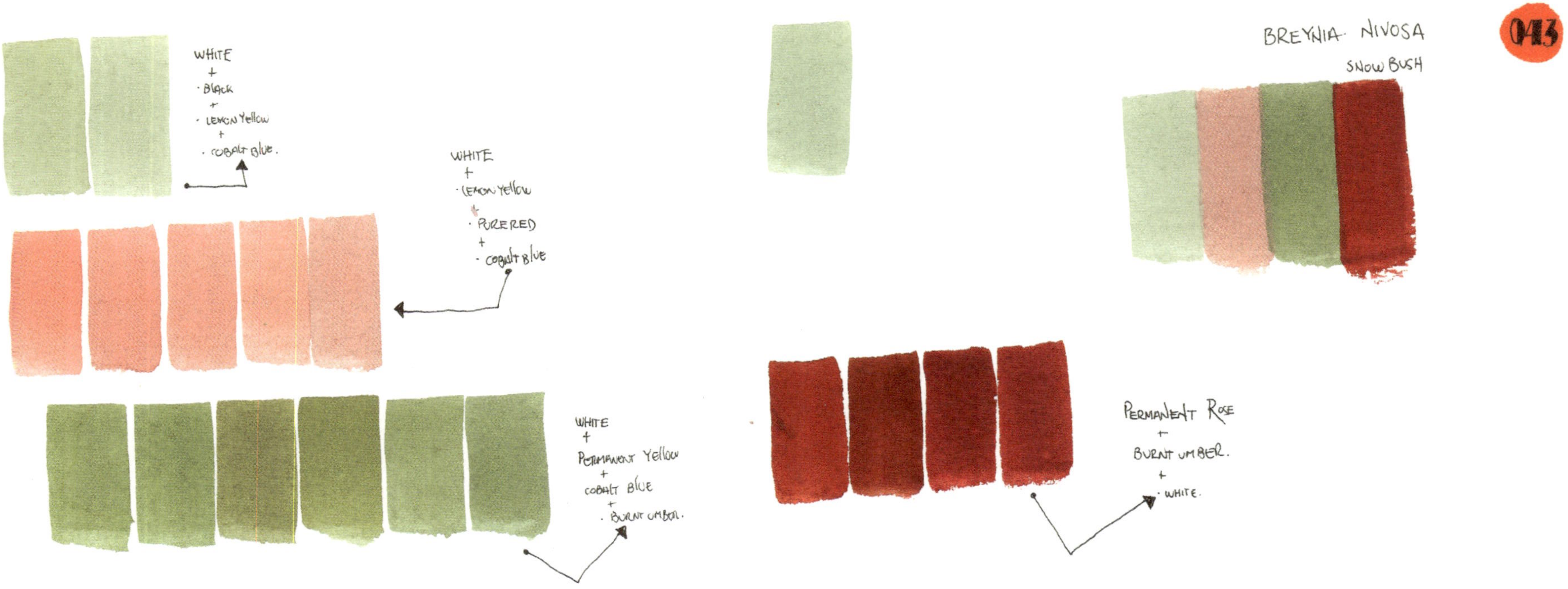
043
BREYNIA NIVOSA
SNOW BUSH
WHITE + BLACK + LEMON YELLOW + COBALT BLUE.
WHITE + LEMON YELLOW + PURE RED + COBALT BLUE
WHITE + PERMANENT YELLOW + COBALT BLUE + BURNT UMBER.
PERMANENT ROSE + BURNT UMBER. + WHITE.

044

CENTRANTUS RUBER ALBUS

JUPITER'S BEARD WHITE

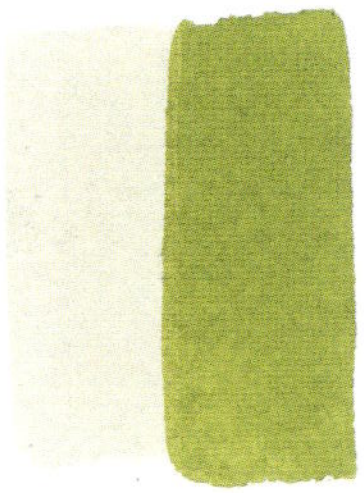

WHITE
+
· LEMON YELLOW ·

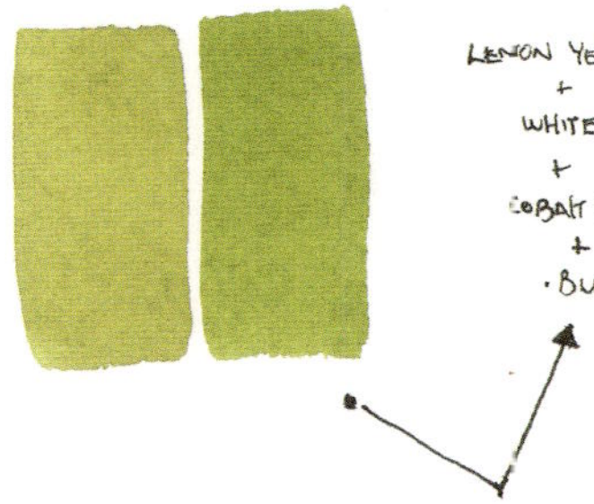

LEMON YELLOW
+
WHITE
+
COBALT BLUE
+
· BURNT UMBER

GAURA LINDHIMERI 045

WHIRLING BUTTERFLIES WHITE.

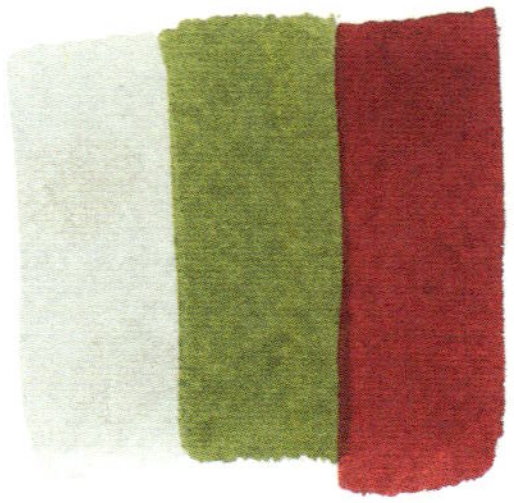

WHITE
+
· COBALT ·
+
· LEMON YELLOW.

LEMON YELLOW
+
ULTRAMARINE
+
+
B. UMBER.
+
· WHITE.

PERMANENT ROSE
+
BURNT UMBER
+
WHITE

046

BOUGAINVILLEA
SAN DIEGO RED

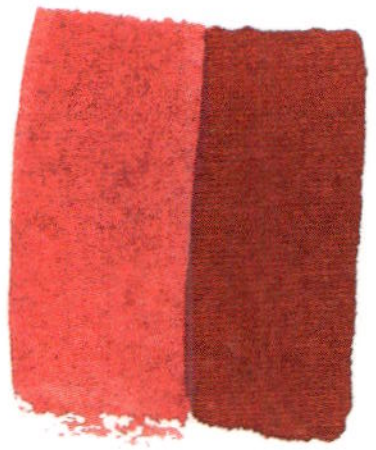

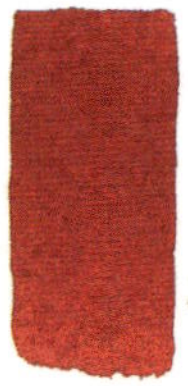

PERMANENT ROSE
+
PURE RED
+
BURNT UMBER
+
· WHITE ·

PERMANENT ROSE
+
WHITE
+
· LEMON YELLOW ·

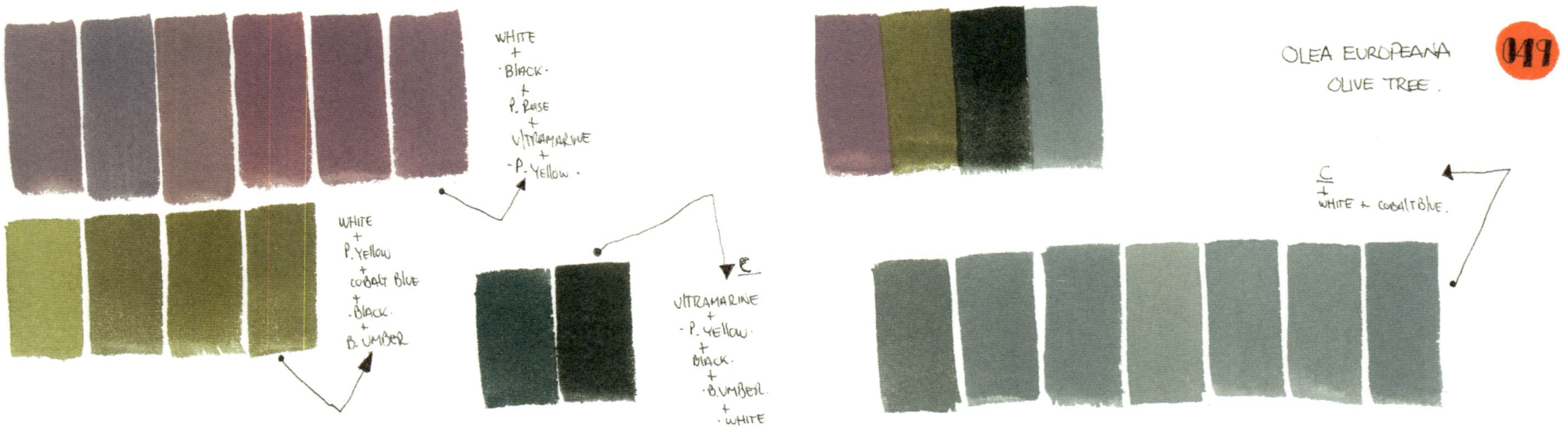
OLEA EUROPEANA
OLIVE TREE.
076
WHITE + BLACK + P. ROSE + ULTRAMARINE + P. YELLOW
WHITE + P. YELLOW + COBALT BLUE + BLACK + B. UMBER
C
ULTRAMARINE + P. YELLOW + BLACK + B. UMBER + WHITE
C + WHITE + COBALT BLUE.

ANGIO ZANTHOS
KANGAROO PAWS RED
050

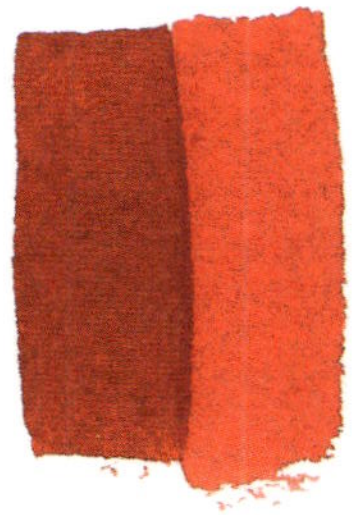

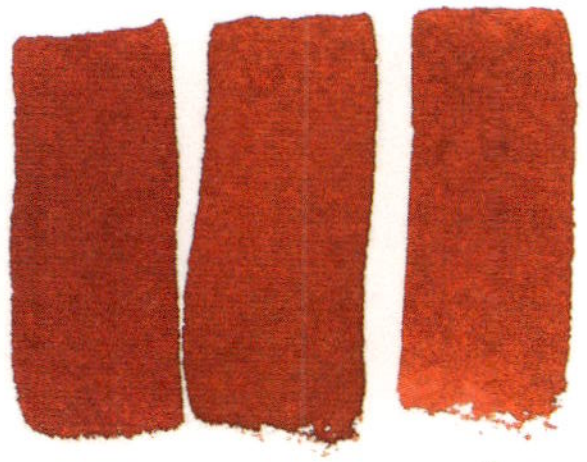

A
PURE RED
+
BURNT UMBER
+
· PERMANENT YELLOW
+
· BLACK + · WHITE ·

A
+
WHITE +
PERMANENT ROSE

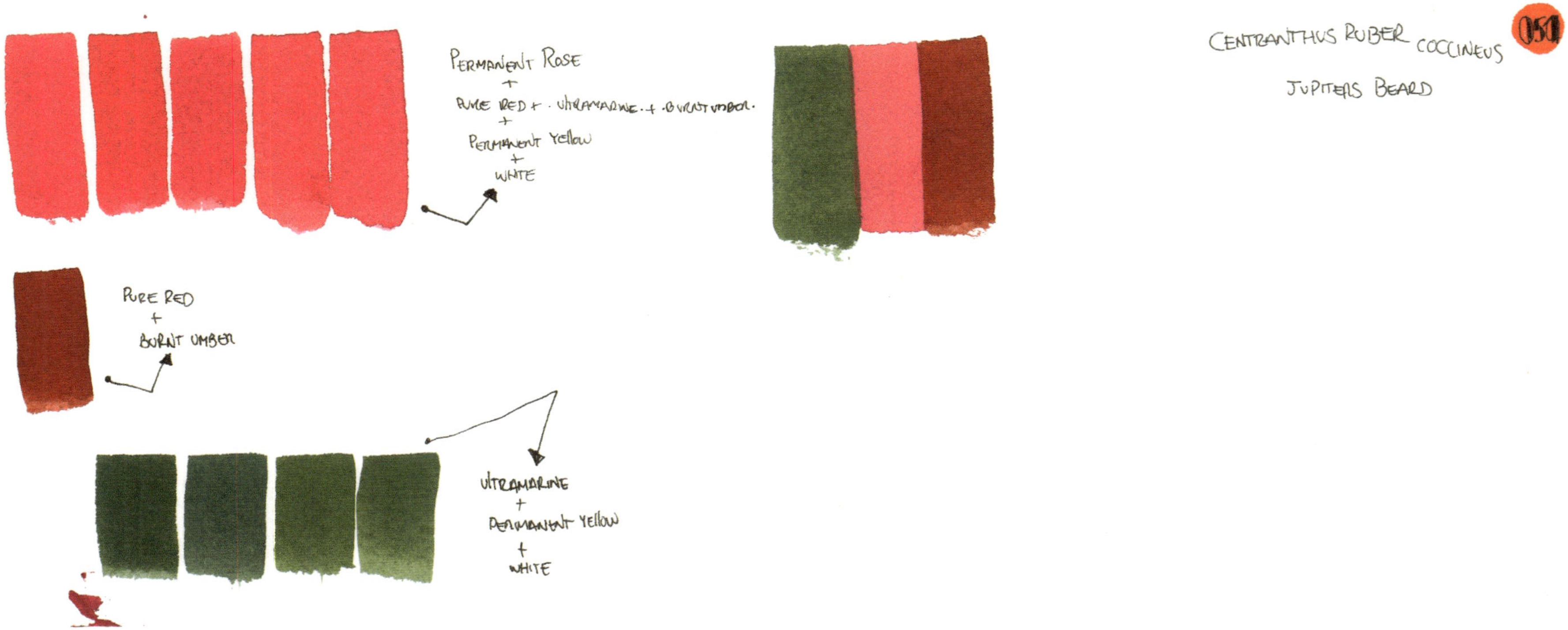
051
CENTRANTHUS RUBER COCCINEUS
JUPITERS BEARD
PERMANENT ROSE
+
PURE RED + ULTRAMARINE + BURNT UMBER
+
PERMANENT YELLOW
+
WHITE
PURE RED
+
BURNT UMBER
ULTRAMARINE
+
PERMANENT YELLOW
+
WHITE

METROSIDEROS EXCELSA 052
NEW ZEALAND CHRISTMAS TREE.

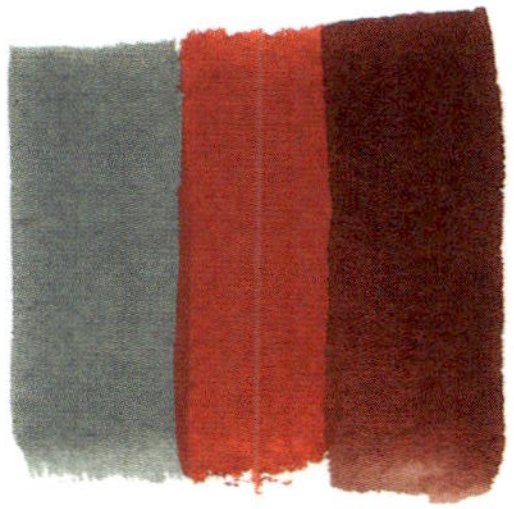

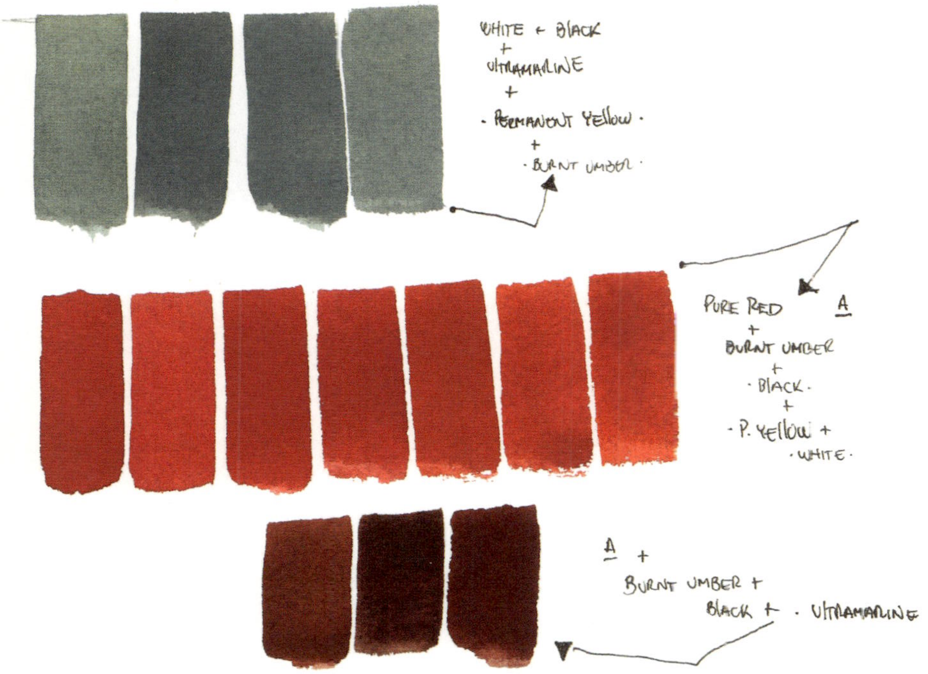

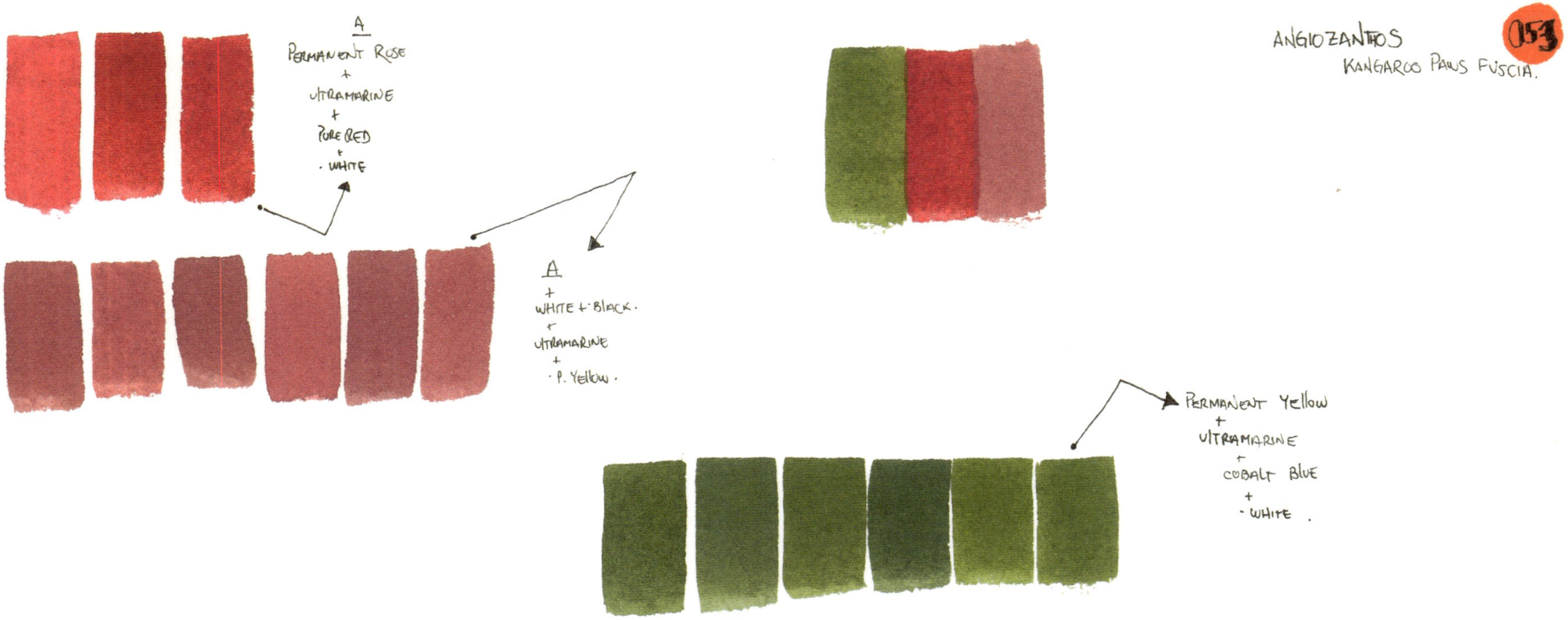
ANGIOZANTHOS
KANGAROO PAWS FUSCIA.
053
A
PERMANENT ROSE
+
ULTRAMARINE
+
PURE RED
+
· WHITE
A
+
WHITE + BLACK.
+
ULTRAMARINE
+
· P. YELLOW.
PERMANENT YELLOW
+
ULTRAMARINE
+
COBALT BLUE
+
· WHITE .

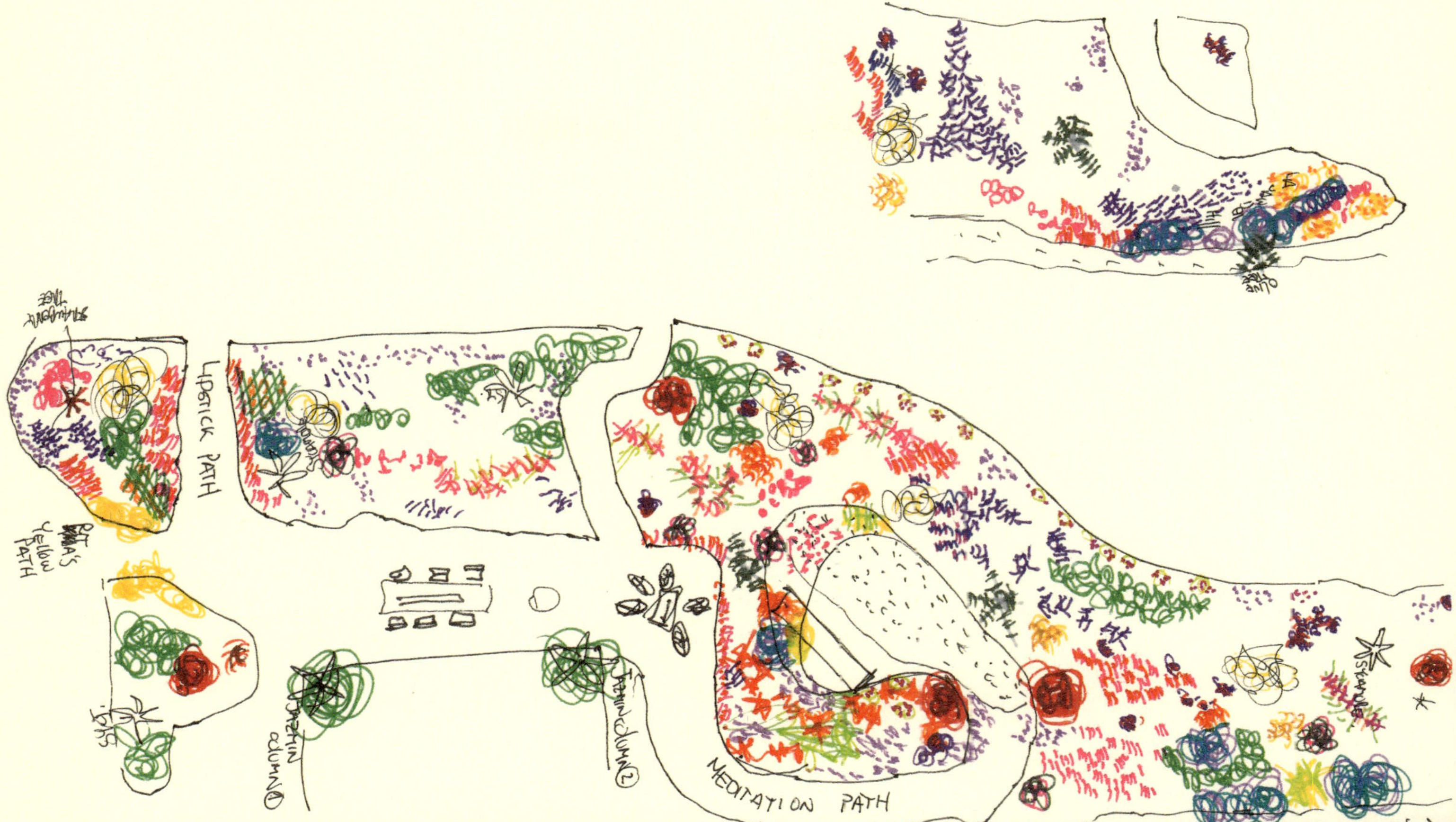
LIPSTICK PATH
MEDITATION PATH
Yellow PATH
COLUMN ①
COLUMN ②
OLIVE TREE

Color sketch of the *haudenschild*Garage garden (2017)

Boceto de color del jardín del *haudenschild*Garage (2017)

TRACHELOSPERUM JASMINOIDES 051
STAR JASMIN

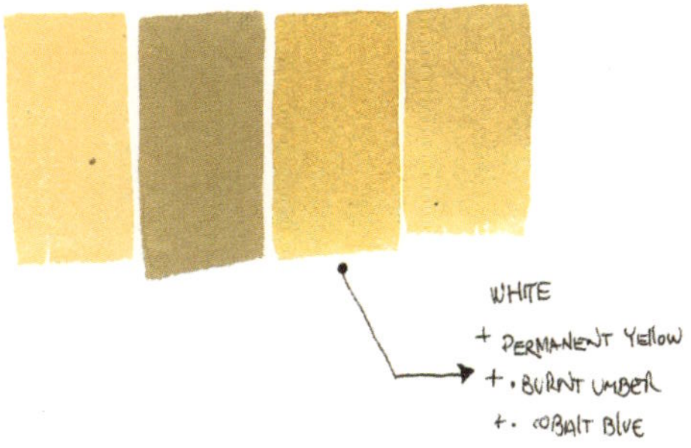

GARDENIA JASMINOIDES 057
EVERBLOOMING GARDENIA
WHITE + · BLACK + · COBALT BLUE + · P. ROSE
B WHITE + · LEMON YELLOW + · B.UMBER·
B + COBALT BLUE + PERMANENT YELLOW + B. UMBER + · WHITE ·

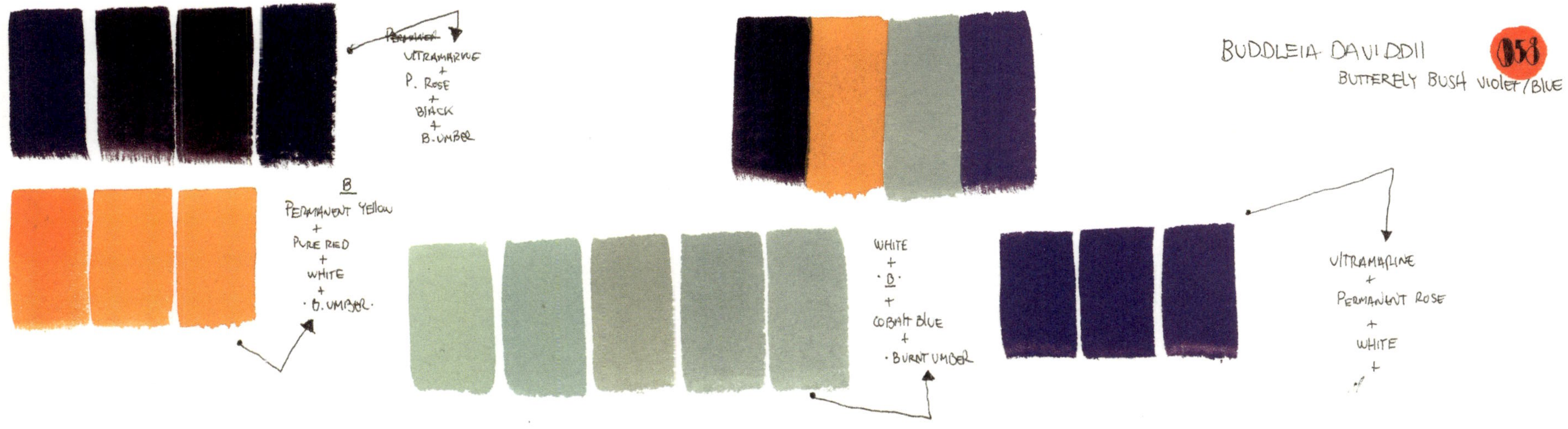

BUDDLEIA DAVIDDII
058
BUTTERFLY BUSH VIOLET/BLUE
ULTRAMARINE + P. ROSE + BLACK + B. UMBER
B
PERMANENT YELLOW + PURE RED + WHITE + ·B. UMBER·
WHITE + ·B· + COBALT BLUE + ·BURNT UMBER
ULTRAMARINE + PERMANENT ROSE + WHITE +

063

TIPUANA TIPO

YELLOW JACARANDA

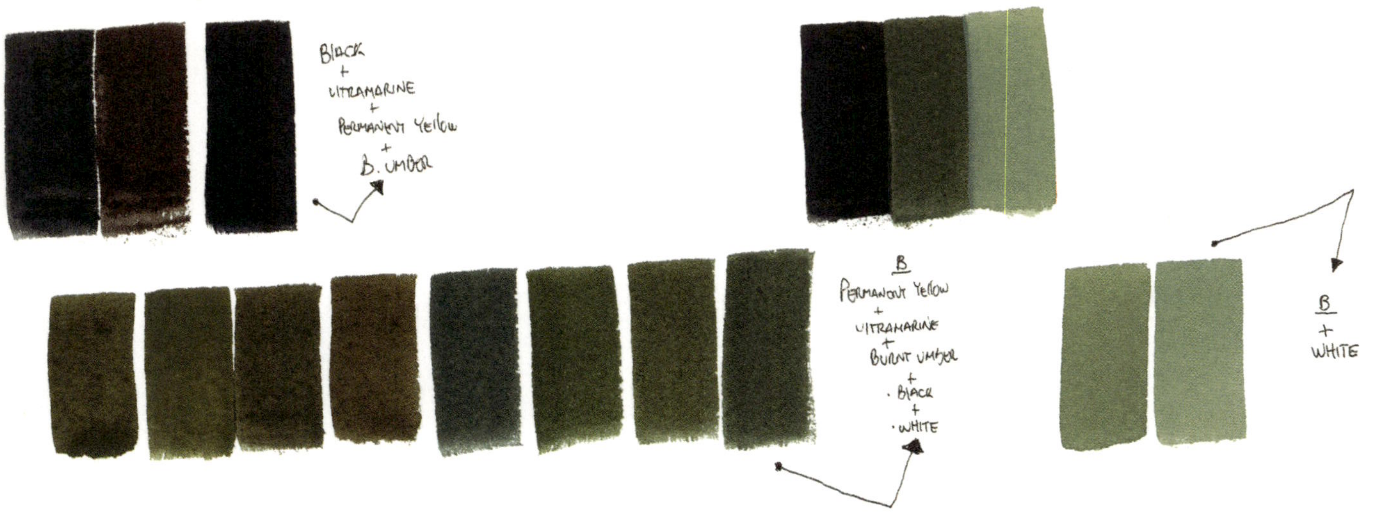

HARPEPHYLLUM CAFFRUM 064

SOUTH AFRICAN PLUM TREE

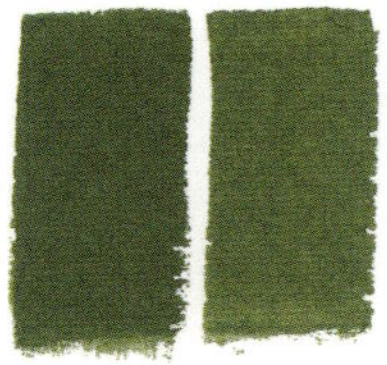

PERMANENT YELLOW
+
COBALT BLUE
+
B. UMBER
+
· WHITE
+
· BLACK.

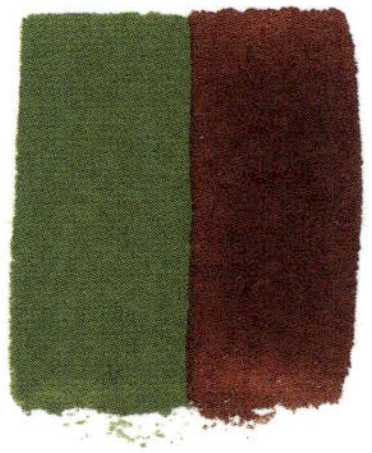

PURE RED
+
BURNT UMBER
+
BLACK
+
· P. YELLOW ·
+
· WHITE.

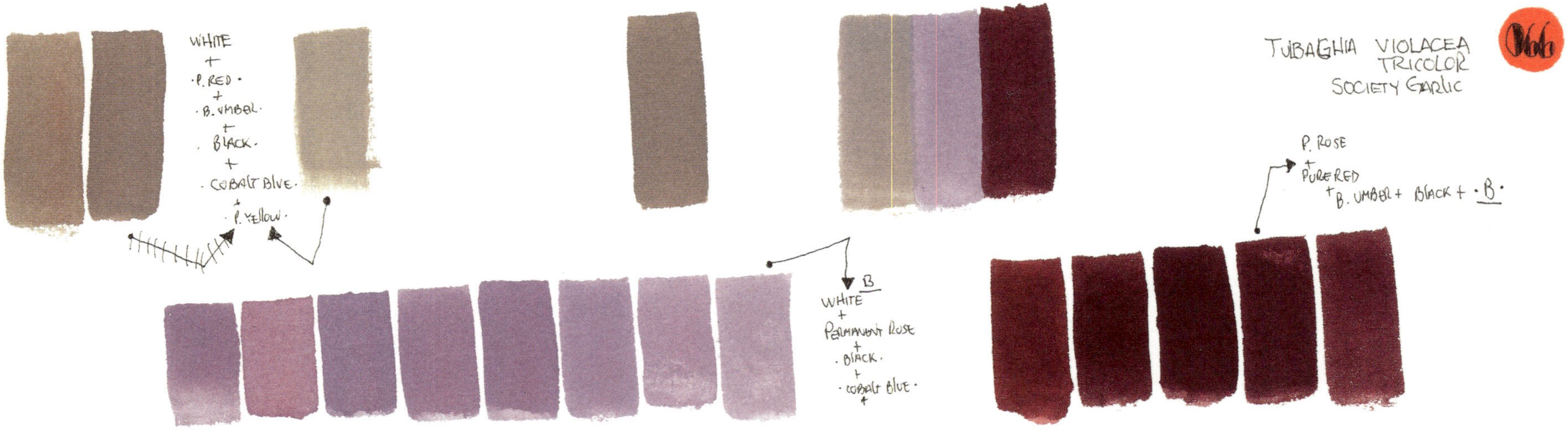
066
TULBAGHIA VIOLACEA
TRICOLOR
SOCIETY GARLIC
WHITE + P. RED + B. UMBER + BLACK + COBALT BLUE + P. YELLOW
B
WHITE + PERMANENT ROSE + BLACK + COBALT BLUE +
P. ROSE + PURE RED + B. UMBER + BLACK + B

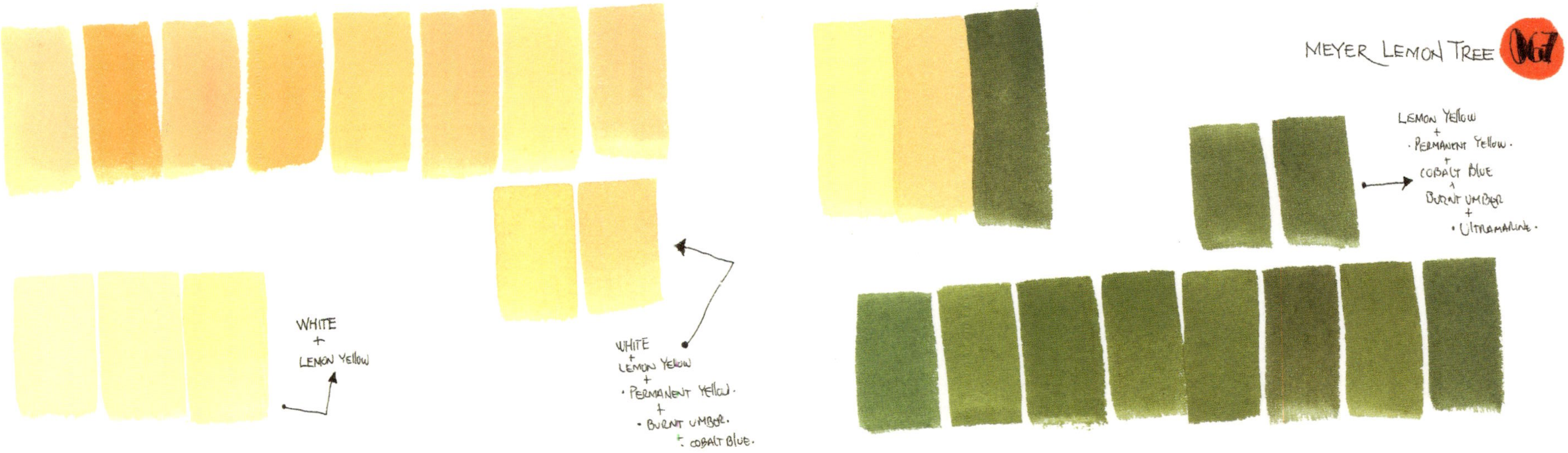
MEYER LEMON TREE
067
LEMON YELLOW + PERMANENT YELLOW + COBALT BLUE + BURNT UMBER + ULTRAMARINE
WHITE + LEMON YELLOW
WHITE + LEMON YELLOW + PERMANENT YELLOW + BURNT UMBER + COBALT BLUE

072

CESTRUM NOCTURNUM

HUELE D NOCHE/
QUEEN OF THE NIGHT

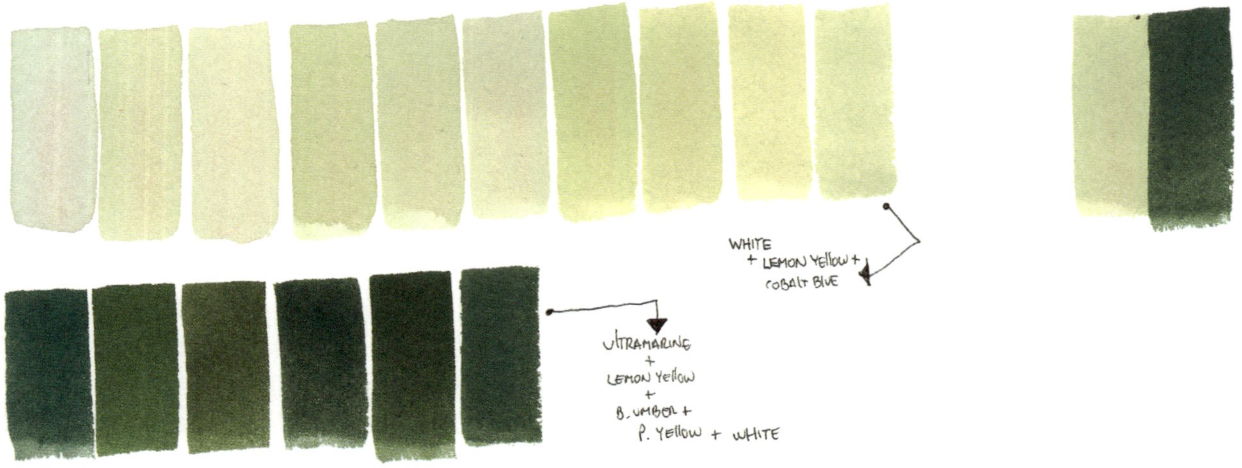

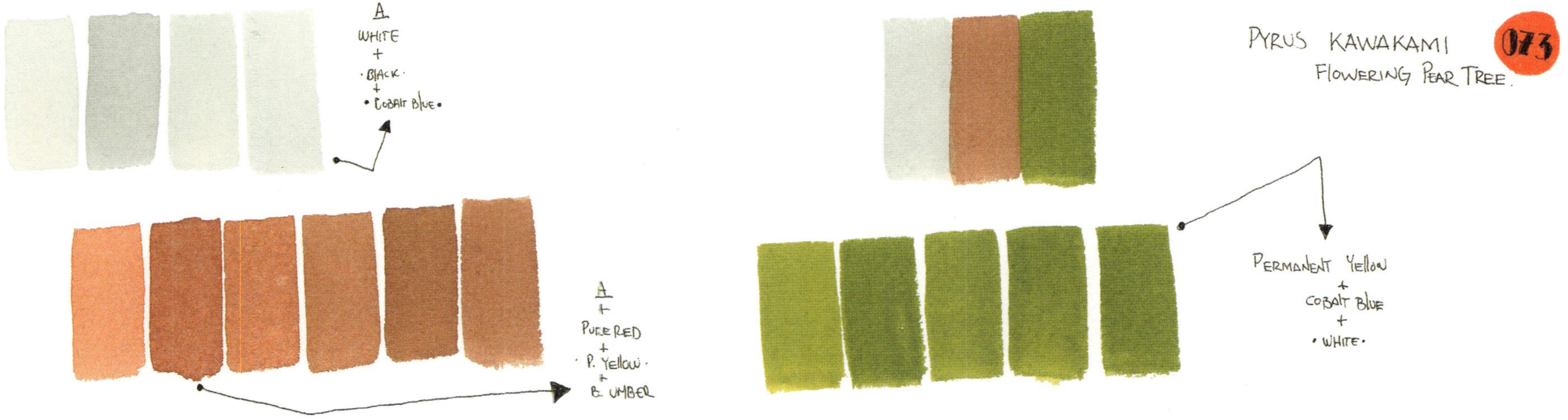

073
PYRUS KAWAKAMI
FLOWERING PEAR TREE.
A
WHITE
+
BLACK
+
COBALT BLUE
A
+
PURE RED
+
P. YELLOW
+
B. UMBER
PERMANENT YELLOW
+
COBALT BLUE
+
WHITE

076

EUPHORBIA MILI

CROWN OF THORNES

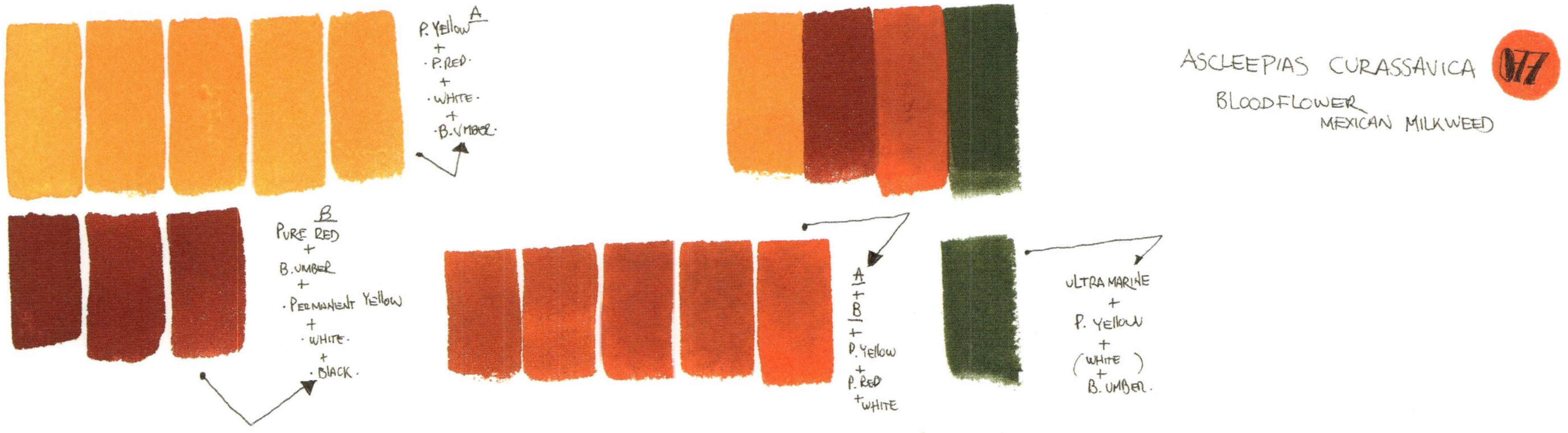
ASCLEEPIAS CURASSAVICA
077
BLOODFLOWER
MEXICAN MILKWEED
A
P. Yellow + P. RED + WHITE + B. UMBER
B
PURE RED + B. UMBER + PERMANENT YELLOW + WHITE + BLACK
A + B + P. Yellow + P. RED + WHITE
ULTRA MARINE + P. YELLOW + (WHITE) + B. UMBER

078 Brachychiton Acerifolia
Australian Flame Tree.

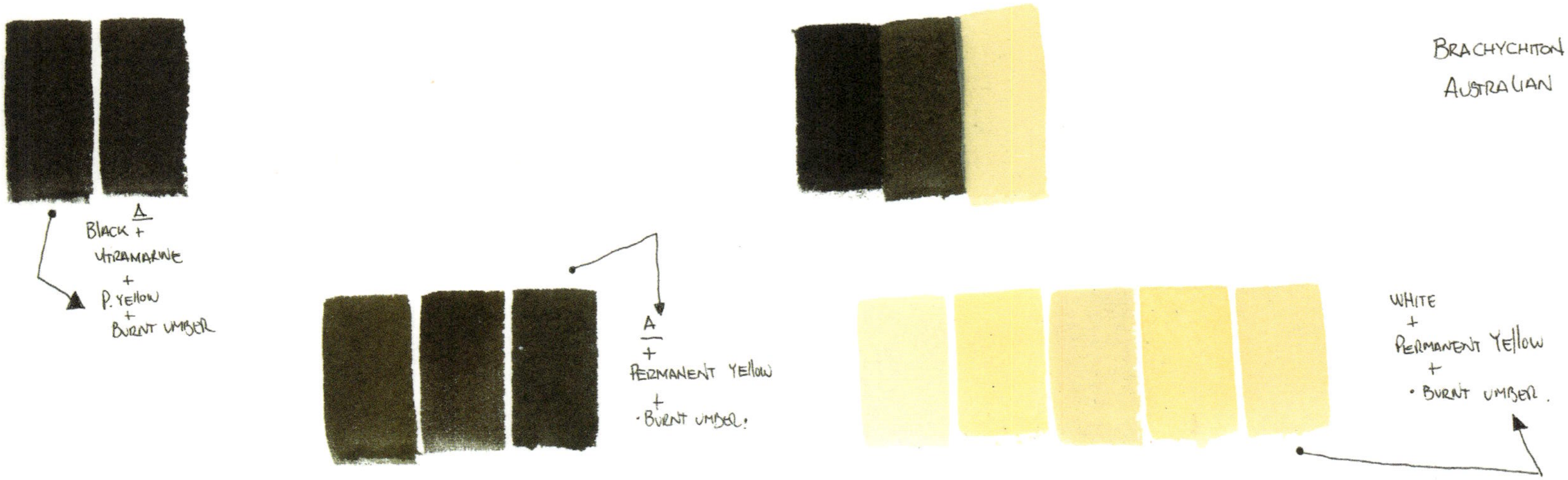

079 DISTICTUS BUCCINATORIA

BLOOD RED TRUMPET VINE

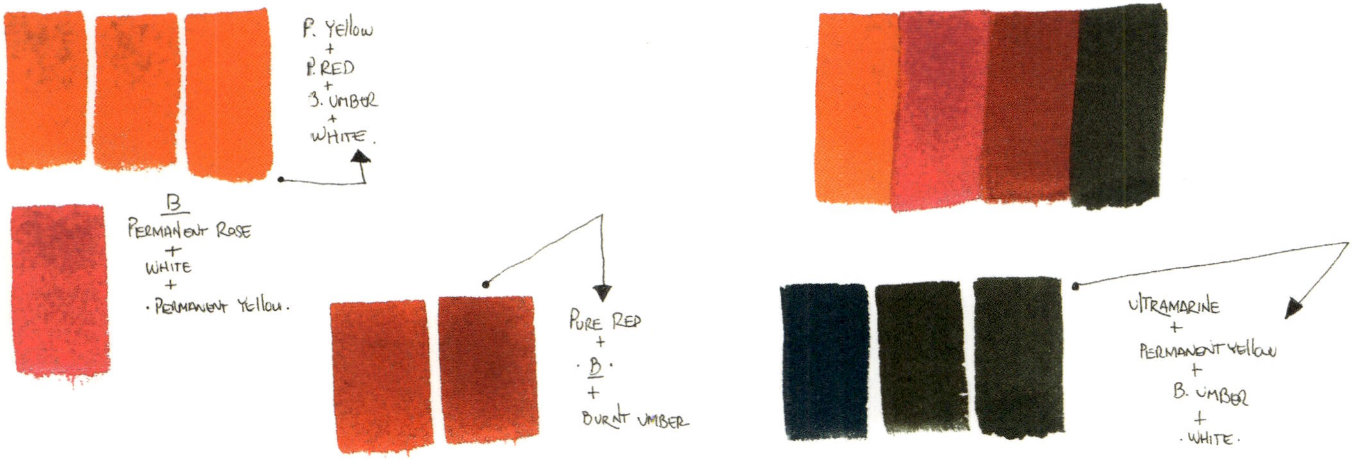

Este texto narra de forma ficcional los encuentros del artista Erick Meyenberg, el diseñador del paisaje Chris Shea y Eloisa Haudenschild de 2015 a 2017, como parte del proyecto *Even When Fall Is Here*, llevado a cabo en el *haudenschild*Garage. El proyecto, comisionado y organizado por Eloisa Haudenschild, toma como escenario el jardín de su casa en La Jolla, San Diego.

El punto de partida de este trabajo es un diario realizado por Chris Shea, diseñador de paisajes que trabajaba desde hacía años con Eloisa Haudenschild. En esas páginas, Shea junta una serie de imágenes del jardín tomadas a lo largo de dos años, con los nombres correspondientes de las plantas, su crecimiento y sus respectivas gamas de colores. Cuando a Shea se le diagnosticó una enfermedad terminal, el diario se convirtió en una guía de éste para Eloisa Haudenschild, con el propósito de mantener el jardín vivo en los años venideros. Al mismo tiempo, este conjunto de imágenes ilustraba en manera significativa el paso del tiempo que le quedaba por vivir.

Tras las primeras conversaciones entre Meyenberg y Shea, el primero se sintió conmovido por la sabiduría y dedicación del diseñador de paisajes, y decidió traducir aquellos colores de las plantas en gamas cromáticas pintadas con gouache, creando una composición abstracta de la guía/diario. Este geometrismo de colores funcionaba como una suerte de partitura, donde el artista reproducía de forma cuasi obsesiva cada una de las manchas cromáticas que aparecen en las fotografías de Shea. La composición de Meyenberg estaba acompañada por fragmentos en blanco, silencios que definían el propio fluir del jardín física y temporalmente.

Este texto de color sirvió como base para un video donde Meyenberg camina con Shea a través del jardín, mientras el jardinero le explica su profusa relación con las plantas. Meyenberg creó un video multicanal con imágenes y sonido para acompañar las palabras de Shea, así como sus pisadas en el jardín. Una pintura performada que describe la historia de un espacio vivo, a partir de la objetividad de los colores. La obra en video fue colocada posteriormente en el jardín de Eloisa Haudenschild durante un solo día, confundiéndose con el propio paisaje.

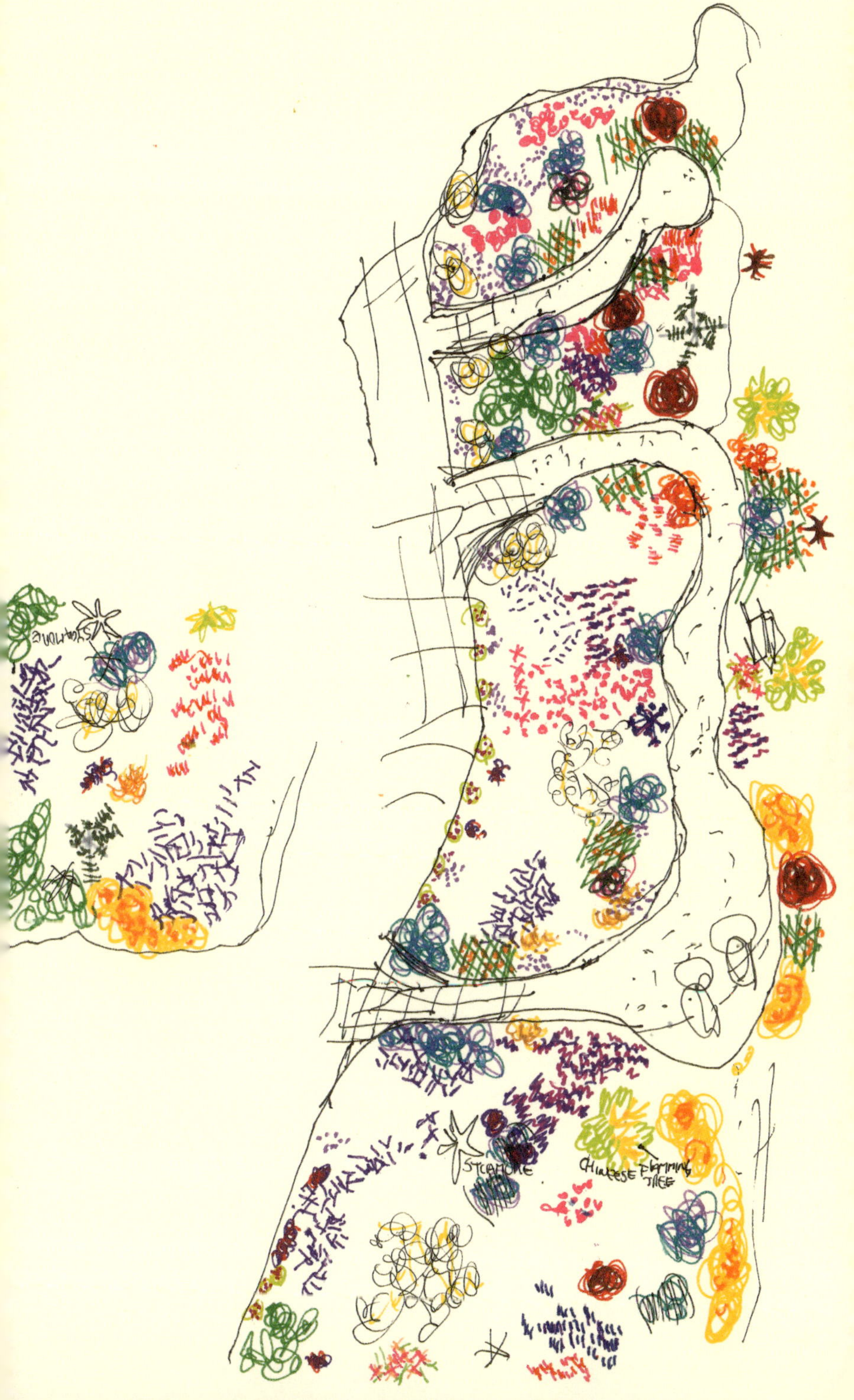
SYCAMORE
SYCAMORE
CHINESE FLAMING TREE

Color sketch of the *haudenschild*Garage garden (2017)

Boceto de color del jardín del *haudenschild*Garage (2017)

Ruth Estévez

Aunque nada de lo aquí descrito es completamente verídico, este texto funciona como un pentagrama para insertar algunas de las notas, diálogos y expresiones que se escribieron, grabaron o simplemente se recordaron para realizar el proyecto. A pesar de la riqueza visual y las múltiples capas que formulan el trabajo de Meyenberg para el *haudenschild*Garage, son las relaciones y las conversaciones personales que se generaron entre los protagonistas las que hilan el contenido de esta narración. Frases que provienen de fuentes subjetivas como los recuerdos de Meyenberg, o notas más precisas, desde los e-mails personales hasta citas sacadas de libros sobre los diferentes aspectos de la historia y las genealogías del jardín, así como textos que reflexionan sobre el uso del lenguaje. Este ejercicio intertextual relaciona a los dos protagonistas de la historia (Meyenberg y Shea), la mentora del proyecto (Haudenschild) y la escritora del texto (Estévez), integrando facultades de unos en los otros, como si se tratase de un personaje múltiple.

Con sinceridad, el jardín era lo que realmente había dado forma a su biografía. Para muchos, este pequeño espacio de tierra desaparecerá con el tiempo como lo hacen siempre las anécdotas (y, posiblemente, solo sobreviva como ruina). La vida pública, sus novelas y poemas y los elogios que lo acompañaron a lo largo de todos aquellos años corren paralelos a esta zona verde. **"Verde claro, verde oscuro"** –diría C., para definirlo en pocas palabras–.[1]

No deja de ser paradójico combinar un currículum dedicado al lenguaje y al mismo tiempo evitar la escritura. O, mejor dicho, dejar de sentirse responsable por el uso que se hace de ella. En cualquier caso, C. estaba comprometido con una vida dedicada a la narración escrita que eventualmente frenaba para dedicarse a otro tipo de mímicas corporales. A la fecha no creo que sean incompatibles las dos cosas.[2] Es en los gestos donde surge/n esta/s historia/s, donde se mezclan el trabajo y una buena dosis de no querer hacer nada. En este jardín, el trabajo esencial [de C.] consistía en distraerse, en pensar en otra cosa, en fantasear, en no apresurarse para irse a dormir.

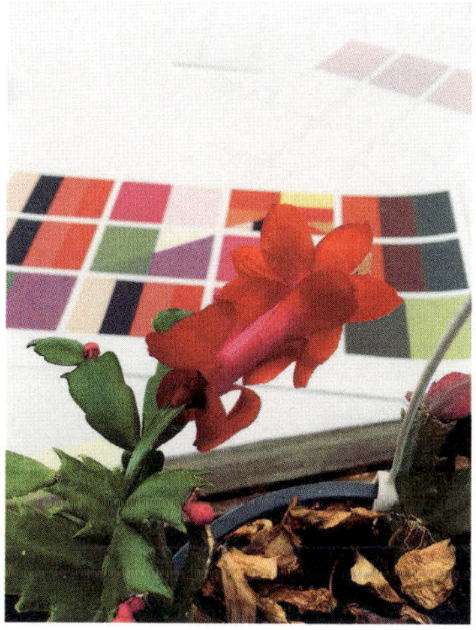

"Me gusta la jardinería", dijo C. **"Es un espacio donde puedo encontrarme cuando necesito perderme".**[3]

Desde fuera, no había lugar para malentendidos, sobre todo porque el jardín de C. era un lugar privado [que no un jardín secreto], donde rara vez entraban los invitados.[4] Al final del lateral del terreno, había un montículo de una buena altura, que dejaba la pared del recinto al nivel del pecho, para poder asomarse a los campos.[5] De hecho, si uno se alejaba varios cientos de metros de aquel "muro" de contención, se veía todo el panorama con tenue claridad. Un ejercicio que, ensayado de forma regular, revelaba los sistemas de colores que se expandían y cambiaban con el tiempo: el jardín era una pradera formada por lechos de perennes y pastos, plantados por miles y en grupos entremezclados. [...] Las combinaciones primero cobran vida dentro de la casa [de C.], donde los lápices de colores se abren camino en el papel dibujando jeroglíficos enigmáticos que se leen como arte.[6] (O al menos así los interpreté).

1 Chris Shea en conversación con Erick Meyenberg, 2015-2017.
2 Fernando Sorrentino, *Siete conversaciones con Jorge Luis Borges* (Buenos Aires: Casa Pardo, 1974).
3 Shea en conversación con Meyenberg.
4 *El jardín secreto* [*The Secret Garden*] (1911) es un clásico de la literatura infantil inglesa escrito por Frances Hodgson Burnett.
5 Francis Bacon, "Of Gardens", en *Essays, Civil and Moral. The Harvard Classics*, vol. 3, parte 1 (New York: P.F. Collier & Son, 1909-14), 181.
6 Adrian Higgins, "A new film takes us inside the mind—and the garden—of Piet Oudolf" [Una nueva película que nos lleva dentro de la mente –y el jardín– de Piet Oudolf"], *The Washington Post*, 20 de marzo, 2018. Web.

A C. le gustaba decir que su jardín era un jardín lateral.[7] No se encontraba a la vera de ningún otro espacio más allá del campo abierto, que estaba igualmente flanqueado por lotes de tierra, parcelas y áreas de cultivo. Sin embargo, esa lateralidad le servía para seguir así, expandiéndose y "cavando hoyos en cualquier lado".[8] C. modificaba las relaciones jerárquicas del jardín. Le entretenía guiarse por esas prácticas consideradas secundarias respecto a la propia creación, como el comentario, la nota, la glosa o la cita le corresponden a la escritura.[9] En realidad, el jardín estaba lleno de muchos espacios adicionales que no se concretaban. Esta operación de desvío era una forma simple de describir un trabajo más o menos intuitivo, donde la técnica se perfilaba a través de las semióticas del calendario.

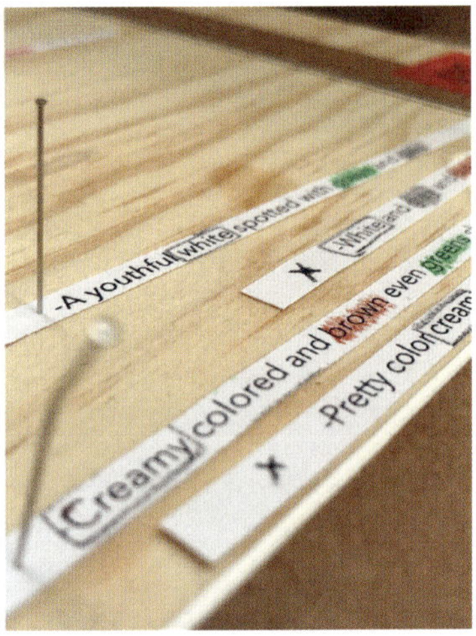

No creo que C., si lo pienso en retrospectiva, hubiera aceptado que usara el jardín, el suyo o cualquier otro, como metáfora de nada. Sin embargo, ahora que me toca hablar de él (del jardín y de C.), no encuentro otra forma de hacerlo. **Estamos demasiado acostumbrados a utilizar el jardín y el ciclo de las plantas bajo la dialéctica de la comparación y el juego de palabras, y resulta complicado deshacerse de ellas.**[10] C. no hacía uso de metáforas, ni hipérbatos, ni nada que exagerara, convirtiera en, o condujera hacia, para hablar de su jardín. Las historias de los lados, como las plantas que crecían en él, no pretendían nada más. **El desinterés que marcaban los colores.**[11]

Después de haber caminado juntos por el jardín durante un par de horas, C. me contó sobre aquella película de 1979 que narra la historia de Chance, un jardinero cuyo única experiencia de vida era el cultivo de su jardín.[12] Me imagino que no se refería a sí mismo, pero nunca supe a ciencia cierta lo que surgía de su memoria o de la invención, o si sus relatos eran fruto de ambas. Puede ser que me estuviera invitando a reflexionar sobre los trucos que se gasta el lenguaje frente a la honestidad de su pequeño pedazo de tierra. Después de un accidente, Chance queda inconsciente y lo recoge una acaudalada pareja que lo bautiza como Chauncey Gardiner, tras malentender su verdadero

7 Bacon, *op. cit.*, 181.

8 Edward de Bono, *Lateral Thinking; Creativity Step by Step* (New York: Harper & Row, 1970), 46.

9 Liliana Weinberg, "Jorge Luis Borges: lectura y escritura", *Revista de Estudios Latinoamericanos* 64 (2017): 71-98.

10 Shea en conversación con Meyenberg.

11 *Idem*.

12 *Being There* (1979), una película dirigida por Hal Ashby y basada en una novela de 1970 escrita por Jerzy Kosiński.

nombre. Gardener se transforma en Gardiner. Gardener por Gardiner, o, mejor dicho, Chance por Chauncey. Chauncey Gardiner. De lo simple a lo sofisticado, de lo azaroso a lo preciso por culpa de un perverso juego de palabras. "¿Lo ves?", dijo C. **"No hay que utilizar el jardín como metáfora de nada para evitar malentendidos, aunque éstos puedan jugar en tu propio beneficio".**[13]

"Bueno, la verdad es que no tengo una forma concreta de describir ese verde", le dije, para protegerme de sus continuas evasivas. "Algo entre verde grisáceo y azul verdoso, ¿no crees?[14] **Tomé un poco de aire al ver que no respondía y me atreví a continuar:** "No hay mejor forma de expresar un sentimiento que a través de un jardín".[15] **"Te equivocas", me interrumpió entonces C.,** "no hay una vulgaridad más grande que un jardín vulgar", **para acabar de contradecirme.**[16] "Cuando hablamos de jardines, o, mejor dicho, cuando tratamos de escribir sobre ellos, el lenguaje está cargado de retórica, y esto tiene que ver, tal vez, con un antecedente literario antiguo".[17] **"¿El paraíso?", pregunté. "La perfección", dijo él. "O al menos la intención de hacer una versión ecológica de un lugar para el descanso y la relajación eterna; el lugar para los músculos flácidos".**

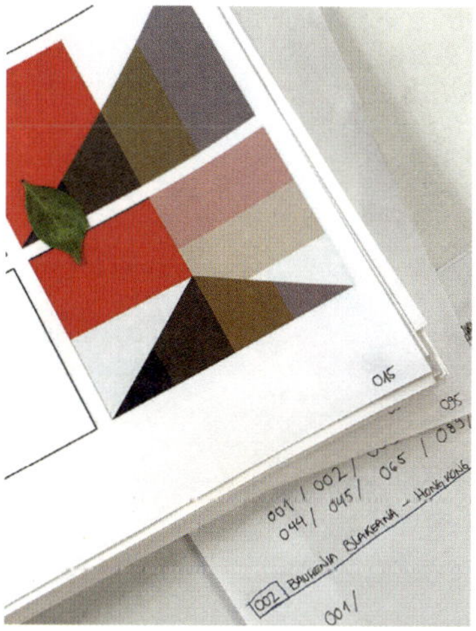

[El jardín] es el mayor placer para el espíritu del hombre; sin lo cual los edificios y palacios no son más que toscas manufacturas; y podrá verse siempre que, cuando las edades avanzan hacia la civilidad y la elegancia, los hombres edifican con belleza antes que hacer jardines delicados; como si la jardinería fuese la mayor perfección.[18]

"Sin embargo", **prosiguió C. después de recordar a Bacon,** "cualquier jardinero, desde aquel que pone un par de macetas en un balcón de un metro cuadrado hasta el comprometido *root-and-baller*, sabe que la jardinería nada tiene que ver con la perfección".[19] **La jardinería como proyecto creativo no se puede lograr porque es un arte que sufre de un déficit de supervivencia orgánica. Me imagino que comunicar el sentido estético de un jardín para aquellos que no estuvieron presentes demanda en primera instancia el uso del lenguaje. Sin duda, un medio**

13 Shea en conversación con Meyenberg.

14 *Idem*.

15 Discurso del arquitecto Luis Barragán para la ceremonia de premiación del Premio Pritzker, martes 3 de junio de 1980. Dumbarton Oaks, Estados Unidos. pritzkerprize.com.

16 Timothy Young, "A Garden Is Not a Metaphor", *JHI Blog*, *Journal of the History of Ideas*, 19 de marzo, 2018. Web.

17 Bacon, *op. cit.*, 211.

18 Bacon, *op. cit.* Edición en español: "De los jardines", en *De la sabiduría egoísta*. Traducción de Luis Escolar Barreño (Editorial Taurus, 2012).

19 Young, *op. cit.*

poco natural y que deja escapar muchas de las pistas de aquello que fue.

"Podemos sustituir directamente las palabras por una paleta de colores", me dijo C., enseñándome una bitácora de instrucciones que había construido durante el transcurso de dos años. Aquel cuaderno mostraba todo tipo de gamas cromáticas que revelaban las diferentes estaciones del jardín a través de los cambios en las plantas. C. no había olvidado escribir los nombres de cada una de ellas, pero se cuidaba de no incluir adjetivos a la ligera.

"Es curioso", me dijo, **"lo rápido que se transforman los nombres de los colores en adjetivos para mejorar el sustantivo que define una flor. A mí me gusta utilizar los colores como sujetos, tomando ventaja de su escasa flexión de género"**.[20]

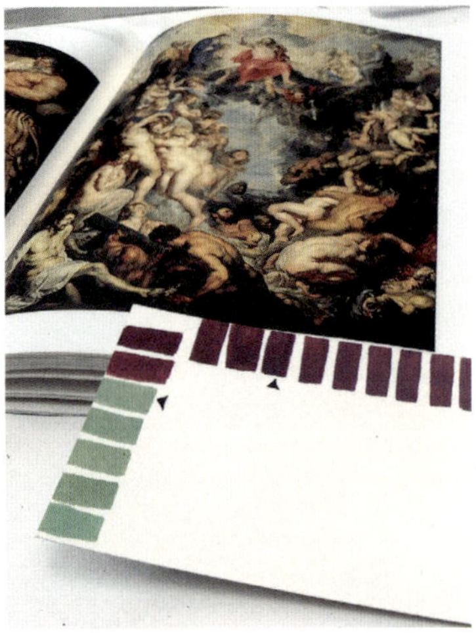

20 Shea en conversación con Meyenberg.

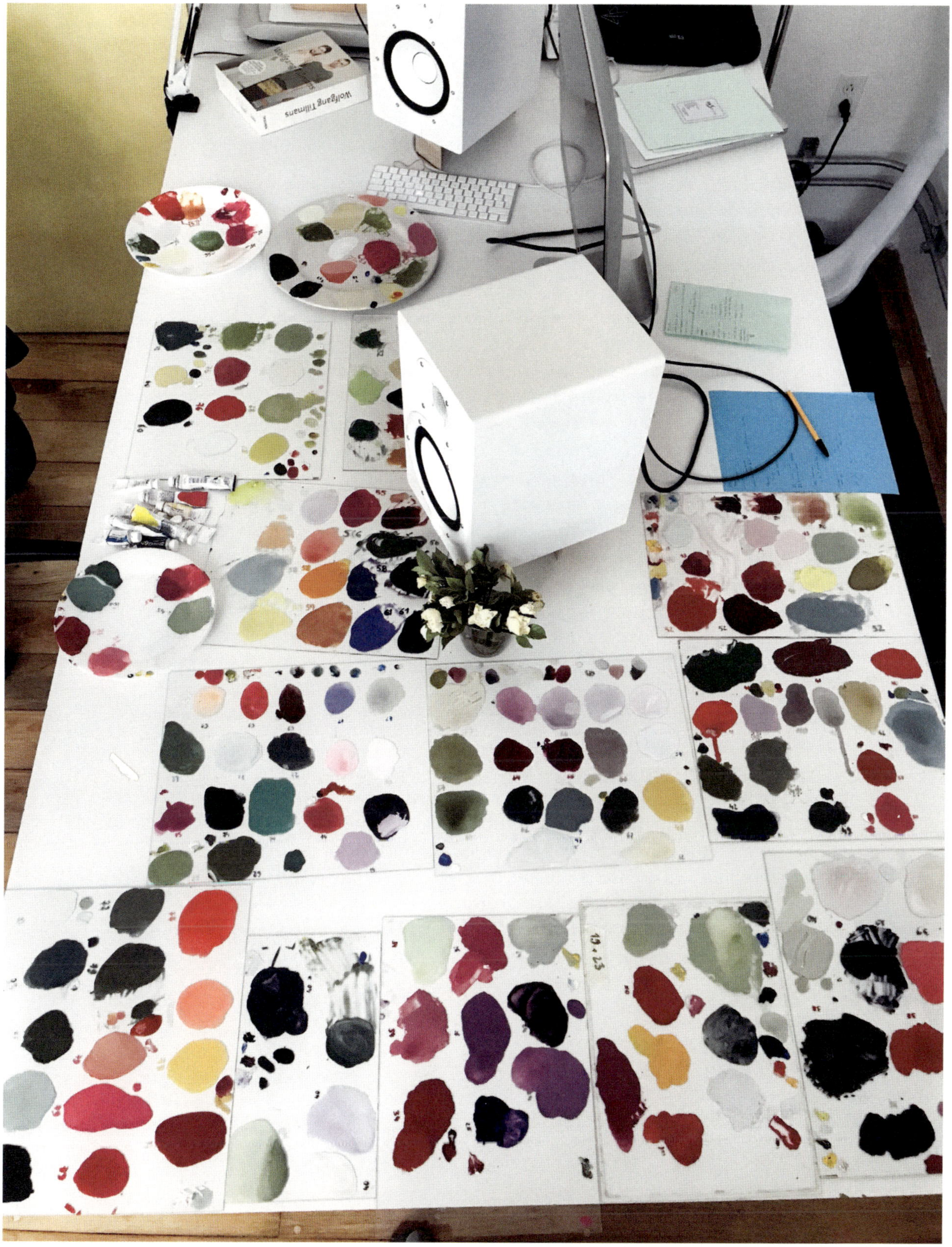
Wolfgang Tillmans

Hola, Eloisa

Te mando una lista de la mayoría de los árboles que tienes en el jardín. Todavía falta incluir algunos arbustos y árboles más grandes. Están enumerados sin un orden particular.

No sé, pensé que sería bueno comenzar por los árboles. Primero puse su genealogía botánica y después el nombre por el que se les conoce comúnmente, el país de origen y la distinción entre hoja perenne, semiperenne o caduca.

Me pareció que ésta era una forma interesante de estimular la discusión sobre la necesidad de utilizar árboles y plantas "nativos" frente a aquellos que se denominan "inmigrantes". Como ves, pocos de nuestros árboles son nativos u originarios de la zona. Sin embargo, muchos son en realidad "inmigrantes", porque se han adaptado bien al entorno y forman parte del paisaje del sur de California desde que me dedico a este trabajo... han estado aquí por generaciones, si no es desde el inicio de la colonización de California.

Categóricamente, las plantas "nativas" son las que existían en California antes de la llegada de los europeos y los colonos a finales del siglo XVIII. Pero en mi mundo, por pequeño que éste sea, considero "nativos" las plantas y los árboles que conozco, con los que he crecido, trabajado y disfrutado durante los últimos cuarenta años de mi vida personal y laboral. En este jardín que hemos creado juntos, muchas de las plantas más deseadas y confiables, y que son clave para este paisaje, serían consideradas como no nativas por los expertos en botánica... pero ése no es mi mundo.

Los árboles y otras plantas con los que he trabajado durante mi vida, los considero "nativos"... o tal vez nativos naturalizados. Ellos han sabido prosperar en esta parte del mundo y son elementos permanentes en nuestro entorno local.

El paisaje que hemos creado no debe responder a una ciencia, se basa en lo mágico. Es una combinación de imaginación, creatividad, sensibilidad y, en este caso, colaboraciones únicas. Agrega a esto un propósito, el amor por los amigos y la familia, y un profundo aprecio por el arte de construir el paisaje al mismo tiempo que el arte que de por sí ya se encuentra en la naturaleza. Se convierte en algo inesperado... y maravilloso.

Esto es solo un comienzo:

Árboles grandes

- *Koelreuteria bipinnata* / Árbol de la llama chino. Nativo de China, Taiwán, Corea. Hoja caduca.
- *Podocarpus gracilior* / Llamado también pino-helecho africano. Nativo del este de África. Hoja perenne.
- *Metrosideros excelsa* / Árbol de navidad neozelandés. Hoja perenne.
- *Platanus x acerifolia* / También conocido como sicómoro de Londres. Hoja caduca.
- *Arbutus "Marina"* / Árbol de fresa. Nativo de Irlanda y el sur de Europa. Hoja perenne.
- *Olea europaea* / Olivo. Considerado como "nativo naturalizado". Hoja perenne.
- *Cinnamomum camphora* / Alcanforero. Nativo de Japón y China. Hoja perenne.
- *Cupaniopsis anacardioides* / Cupania de hoja de anacardo. Nativo del este y el norte de Australia. Hoja perenne.
- *Fraxinus uhdei* / Fresno silvestre mexicano. Nativo de México. Hoja perenne.
- Bauhinia purpurea / Árbol de orquídea púrpura. Nativo del sur de China. Hoja perenne.
- *Tipuana tipu* / Conocido como tipa, tipa blanca o tipuana palo rosa. Nativo de Bolivia y extendido por Sudamérica. Hoja caduca.

Árboles pequeños /Arbustos grandes

- *Euphorbia cotinifolia* / Lechero rojo. Nativo de México, Venezuela y Perú. En nuestro clima es de hoja caduca.
- *Cotinus coggygria* / Árbol del humo, también conocido como árbol del humo púrpura. Nativo de una zona grande del sur de Europa y Asia central, los Himalayas y el norte de China. Hoja caduca.
- *Cercidium "Museo del Desierto"* / Palo verde, también conocido como *Parkinsonia "Museo del Desierto* Nativo de África y Australia. Hoja caduca.
- *Caesalpinia gilliesii* / Ave del paraíso, también conocido como barba de chivo. Esta planta es nativa de la América del Sur, sobre todo Argentina y Uruguay. Se ha naturalizado en Texas y se puede ver en muchas áreas del sudoeste de Estados Unidos. Hoja caduca.
- *Pyrus kawakamii* / Árbol de pera floreado. Nativo de Taiwán. A diferencia del *Pyrus* y otras variedades, este árbol ha generado su propia especie. Los dos que tenemos en el jardín son en espaldera.[21]

21 E-mail de Chris Shea a Eloisa Haudenschild, 2017.

Nos vimos muchas veces durante los siguientes dos años, en diferentes estaciones. Teníamos una buena relación, aunque confieso que solo lo llegué a ver en su jardín. Me pregunto qué habría pasado si nos hubiéramos encontrado en cualquier otro lugar. Por ejemplo, nunca lo vi dentro de aquella casa. Él consideraba la casa y el jardín como iguales, dos elementos que debían ser complementarios, por lo que no veía la necesidad de entrar en el edificio.[22] "¿Es tu casa un espejo del jardín?", me aventuré a preguntarle en una ocasión para ver si me invitaba a entrar. C. empezó a explicarme entonces sobre su hogar a partir de lo que veía por la ventana, para mantenerme literalmente fuera. **"Cuanto más te acercas, mejor lo ves"**, me confesó.[23]

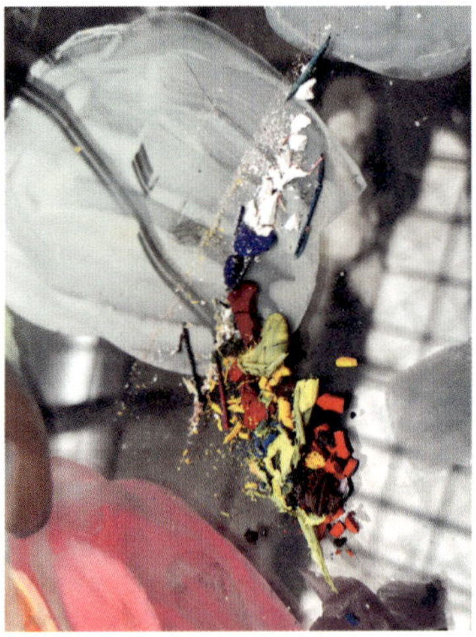

Decidí visitarlo en estaciones diferentes, quizás esperando que me contara sobre sus nuevas ideas y disposiciones en el jardín, o quizás fuera por aquello de mis depresiones. **"Y podemos ver la siguiente generación aquí abajo dispuesta a florecer. Y en este otro lado, se puede ver uno de esos accidentes maravillosos, donde estamos esperando que otra planta crezca".**[24] A pesar de su parsimonia para hablarme del tiempo, como cualquier jardinero, la expectación era parte de C. "Mezclé miles de plantas perennes entre las hierbas, y el resultado es esa vida que fluye entre los espacios que existen entre el lecho de tierra, los límites del tiempo y, sobre todo, en los contornos de [mi] imaginación".[25] "¿Hay acaso lugar para la decepción?", le pregunté.

C. solía pensar mucho en el pasado como un presente continuo. Por mi parte, me sentía incapaz de reconocer sus profecías o recuerdos en ese pasado-presente. Tuve que acostumbrame a improvisar de memoria, ya que el tiempo era una constante en nuestras conversaciones. "La era de las plantas artificiales, realistas, no perecederas, baratas, libres de polen, flexibles, fáciles de obtener, socialmente aceptadas, lavables, ha llegado",[26] dijo inesperadamente un día. Pensé obviamente en la efervescencia del polietileno. Ni siquiera me puedo imaginar a C. rodeado de glicinas artificiales. Probablemente, quería recordarme la importancia del jardín vivo [no estoy seguro

22 Chakceel Rahen, citado en Sally Wilson, "Luis Barragán's Universal Garden", *The Planthunter* 16, 25 de febrero, 2015. Web.
23 Shea en conversación con Meyenberg.
24 *Idem*.
25 Higgins, *op. cit.*
26 S/f, "The Flowering Of Fake Flowers", *The New York Times*, 23 de agosto, 1964. Web.

si de la naturaleza como tal] en la vida de los hombres, utilizando este escenario vegetal como único espacio posible. Aquello me hizo pensar en Chance Gardener. ¿O en Chauncey Gardiner? De cualquier forma, nunca habíamos caminado juntos por las calles de la ciudad, ni habíamos tomado café frente a una jardinera plastificada. Tampoco me había regalado un ramo de flores. C. no arrancaba las plantas hasta que las tenía que arrancar. No obstante, era una persona empática. ¿Acaso no podía serlo una persona a la que le gusta tomarse el tiempo para averiguar si un grupo de begonias tiene sed?

> And coldly the birch leaves are opening one by one.
> Coldly I observe them and wait for the end.
> And it ends.[27]
>
> [Y fríamente las hojas de abedul se van abriendo una por una.
> Con frialdad las observo y espero que llegue el final.
> Y el final llega].

"No creo", dijo C. El tiempo pasa "y **sabes qué, está bien tocar a las plantas,** porque te das cuenta de que no se ofenden".[28] Yo solía ser tímido cuando las tocaba. Las arrancaba al caminar distraído por el camino o, por el contrario, evitaba rozarlas (la mayor parte del tiempo) por miedo a que se descompusiesen. Todo tenía que ver con el profundo distanciamiento que tenía con ellas, mi obsesión irreversible de describirlas con palabras. **"Saber lo que sienten, si están hambrientas o sedientas, con tan solo tocarlas".**[29]

C. era un hombre increíblemente táctil, y eran sus manos las que tomaban verdadera acción en la conversación. **Me di cuenta de que tenía un lenguaje corporal particular cuando se acercaba las plantas, danzando entre las formas, las texturas y los tamaños a través del jardín.**[30] Con el tiempo empecé a darme cuenta de que no era en realidad tan conversador. Su voz podría haber sido el producto de mi falta de atención o una simple ilusión sonora. Empecé a imaginarme **un jardín en múltiples canales, una suerte de coro recitativo.**[31] No era mi pretensión hacer una traducción de sus colores a mis palabras, solo una breve observación sobre el paso del tiempo y la simultaneidad del cambio de ritmos dentro de su jardín.

27 William Carlos Williams, *Early Poems* (Mineola, NY: Dover Publications, 1997), 55.
28 Shea en conversación con Meyenberg.
29 *Idem.*
30 Extracto de un e-mail de Erick Meyenberg a la autora.
31 *Idem.*

Durante los meses de octubre, noviembre y diciembre, dejé de visitarlo. Me imagino que él continuó dibujando en su cuaderno personal. El tiempo siguió haciendo estragos en el jardín y en C. Cuando por fin regresé, me sentía decaído, alterado, y le pregunté si él pensaba que mis depresiones tenían que ver con el cambio de estación. "Es poco probable", dijo, sin prestar demasiada atención. "El porcentaje de la población que se ve afectada por el cambio estacional es tan poco que yo lo descartaría como una hipótesis sólida. En realidad, es mucho más fácil que todo esto. **Ya verás, se ven mejor cuando los atraviesa la luz**", me dijo, señalando a una parte remota del jardín.[32] "Todo es cuestión de iluminación, **una gran luz reflectora**".[33] Es curioso, lo había oído hablar tantas veces del paso de las estaciones que no cuestioné su autoridad. "No te preocupes, no te voy a abandonar en esto. Tendremos que seguir evaluando el porqué de toda esa incertidumbre. Pero no les eches la culpa a mis plantas".

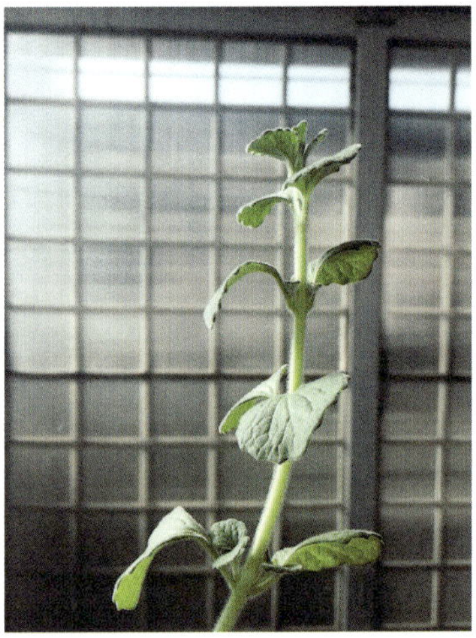

32 Shea en conversación con Meyenberg.

33 *Idem*.

Todo tiene su momento oportuno; hay un tiempo para todo lo que se hace bajo el cielo:

un tiempo para nacer, y un tiempo para morir;
un tiempo para plantar, y un tiempo para cosechar;
un tiempo para matar, y un tiempo para sanar;
un tiempo para destruir, y un tiempo para construir;
un tiempo para llorar, y un tiempo para reír;
un tiempo para estar de luto, y un tiempo para saltar de gusto;
un tiempo para esparcir piedras, y un tiempo para recogerlas;
un tiempo para abrazarse, y un tiempo para despedirse;
un tiempo para intentar, y un tiempo para desistir;
un tiempo para guardar, y un tiempo para desechar;
un tiempo para rasgar, y un tiempo para coser;
un tiempo para callar, y un tiempo para hablar;
un tiempo para amar, y un tiempo para odiar;
un tiempo para la guerra, y un tiempo para la paz.[34]

"En el idioma francés", dijo C., "se usa la expresión '*être de saison* [estacional]', con el significado de 'ser apropiado'". Todo aquello que no es estacional rehúsa la relación con el tiempo.

"No creo que las cosas sean consecuencia unas de otras. Mi experiencia", dijo C., "es armar grupos de forma simultánea y ver el resultado de esas combinaciones. Los resultados siempre son a destiempo. Existe la posibilidad de dejar crecer las plantas a su libre albedrío y no cortarlas nunca, o dejar simplemente que perezcan, sin ayudarlas a renacer". C. no paraba de hacer cosas en ese jardín, pero le molestaba cuando le preguntaban sobre las plantas secas.

La batalla entre la belleza y la no belleza es la hoja de vida de un jardinero. Pienso en todas aquellas cosas que se te escapan de las manos, que perecen y dejan de estar en buen estado. "¿Como un cadáver?", le pregunté. "¿Qué pasa cuando un manojo de flores se convierte en hierba seca?". Me contestó con otra pregunta. Me di cuenta entonces de que todas las composiciones de C. estaban dentro de ese período de declive que sucede a finales de septiembre y principios de noviembre.[35] "A mí me gustan las plantas y también la muerte. Las plantas secas me ayudan a recordar que el jardín es también un trozo de naturaleza.

34 Eclesiastés 3:1/8.
35 Higgins, *op. cit.*

Sin embargo, no creo que el jardín tenga que ser algo que esté relacionado con el paisaje. En realidad, es una habitación donde entras y descubres una cierta intimidad.[36] Cuando cortas una planta porque está seca, es porque deseas su ausencia. Peor aún si quieres cubrir el hueco de forma inmediata".

"Eso suena a una verdadera metáfora sobre la pérdida", le dije, tratando de interrumpirlo. "Para nada", dijo C. "No es sobre la muerte (las plantas volverán a nacer de nuevo en la primavera), pero es esta decadencia que llena el jardín la que me parece más interesante.[37] La gente compra plantas artificiales porque no quiere estar a merced del desvanecimiento de una flor".[38]

En algún momento fui a visitarlo sin previo aviso. Creo que a C. no le gustaba que llegase y lo encontrase fuera, lejos del jardín. "Ahora bien", me comentó, siguiendo la conversación donde la habíamos dejado algunos meses antes, "también existen las estaciones parásitas, aquellas que hacen agujeros o bolsillos en el tiempo. En esa estación no me vas a encontrar, por mucho que vengas a visitarme".[39]

Es extraño que C. hubiera dicho "agujero" o "bolsillo", como si ambas palabras fueran sinónimos. El bolsillo esconde las cosas en el abrigo, pero las retiene ahí, calientes, jugando y moviéndose entre los dedos, hasta que salen de nuevo o se desmenuzan para fundirse con la propia tela. También producen sorpresa cuando uno encuentra lo que daba por perdido. El agujero es algo muy diferente; las cosas se guardan para perderse y ya no se pueden encontrar. Y quizás de ahí el problema de los vacíos, y también de mis depresiones. Prefiero pensar que C. está en esa estación parásita, más cerca de un bolsillo –una estación que podría tomar el nombre de una lectura, de la música, de hacer el amor–.[40] Quiero pensar que ésa es la razón por la que ya no hablamos. Otra experiencia, una temporalmente anacrónica, que se genere alrededor de espacios reales e irreales, lugares para la relajación, campos rodeados de un entorno lingüístico "amniótico" de nidos o islas.[41]

Me pregunto entonces si éstos son los espacios donde está C. cuando no está conmigo o grafiteando su bitácora. Lugares que no tienen presencia física, ni trabajo. Pensé que estaría enredado en algún otro bolsillo, tocándolo todo, como hacía con sus plantas. Me surge, pues, la duda de si para C. yo estoy en un bolsillo o en un agujero.

36 *Idem.*
37 *Idem.*
38 *The New York Times*, *op. cit.*
39 Pascal Quignard, "La quinta estación", en *Albucius* (Los Angeles: Lapis Press, 1993), 55.
40 Quignard, *Idem.*, 56.
41 *Idem.*

Curiosamente, y a pesar de su negación a crear largas descripciones, no puedo dejar de ver en aquel jardín de C. un gran verso sin palabras. En aquella bitácora de imágenes, cada segmento de color alargado parecía una síncopa dentro de la partitura. Si pensamos en los segmentos resultantes de la estructura poética (tetrámetro, pentámetro, etc.), [el jardín de C.] podría ser escaneado como un poema.[42] Me tomé la molestia de agrupar todas las notas que acompañaban las líneas por grupos de colores, dejando solo las palabras. Tal vez no fuese una idea tan acertada, porque las palabras volvieron a distanciarme del jardín.

Pero C. me dejó hacer.

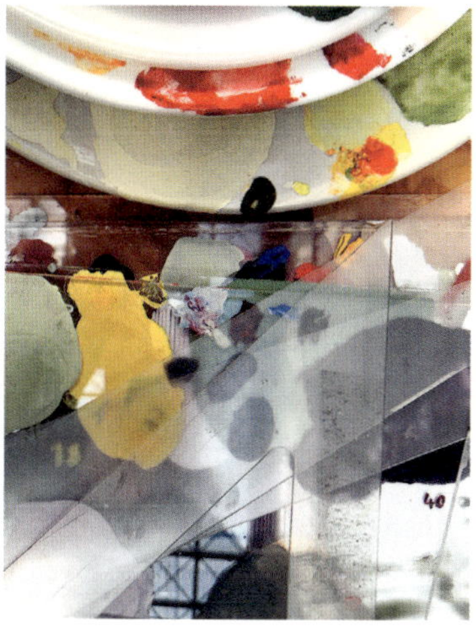

42 Paul Auster, "Black on White: Recent Paintings by David Reed", en *The Art of Hunger: Essays, Prefaces, Interviews, and The Red Notebook* (New York: Penguin Books, 1992), 400.

ROJO: Rojo y blanco, ardiente y firme rojo y naranja / Los nuevos brotes son rojos... los nuevos tallos son rojos y apenas, apenas verdes / El rojo juvenil de una hoja nueva, salpicado entre las hojas verde, amarillento / Es un rojo y verde simplemente indescriptible y... / Verdaderas espigas de rojo y verde, los brotes nuevos de la hoja roja / Manto de rojo y fucsia y manchas de blanco y hojas teñidas de verde y rojo / Rodeadas por esos intensos rojos aterciopelados / Incluso tallos rojos debajo / De nuevo con esas vetas rojas / Y las flores son... eh... de una especie de rojo ladrillo o incluso color coral / Ese rojo vivo es... es como un... / Ésta tiene rojos y rosados y verdes, y muy brillantes, casi como barnizados / Y tallos rojos con brotes nuevos / Y las flores se vuelven rojas y blancas / Ésta recién, está saliendo de la estación fría, así que tiene mucho rojo y un poco de su verde natural, pero va a decolorarse y combinar rosados, y verdes claros, y hasta un poco de blanco / Solo algunos rosados y rojos muy oscuros, e incluso puedes ver que aquí hay algo de blanco o crema / ¿Cuántos tonos de rojo y cobre hay? / Y hay nuevamente algo de ese rojo aquí / ¿O un solo tono de rojo? / Hay un rojo, y también tendrán una pizca de amarillo o anaranjado / Y ésta tiene el rojo, un poquito de casi bermellón, y amarillo y anaranjado / Sabes, va del colorado al azul, y luego a los blancos / Una especie de franja rojiza / Más impresionantes cuando son completamente rojas / Tantas plantas tienen eso, ¿sabes?, nuevos brotes con ese rojo / Rojo vivo / Es un rojo espectacular, muy intenso y aterciopelado / Es un fucsia realmente, realmente inusual, rojo... no estoy seguro de cómo llamarlo / Rojo bermellón sobre un color crema / Empiezan con este rojo y luego se vuelven verdes / Éste es uno que te engaña, aparece el rojo y después surge ese amarillo brillante, brillante / Éste es un bermellón / Sabes, simplemente brotan con un rojo o, en realidad, a veces, un bermellón muy, muy oscuro, y rosados / ¿Puedes ver cómo el sol pasa a través de él, y los rojos y los anaranjados? / Mientras el otro va a volver al rojo / Pero el brote nuevo es rojo / El brote nuevo se ve rojo / Un ramo de la naturaleza, un perfecto arreglo de rojo y verde / El rojo y blanco de la salvia, casi sonriente / Una sombrilla de rojo / Espigas de un rojo magnífico / Algunos brotes nuevos, el rojo y el verde / Cubierta aterciopelada, roja / Rojo muy oscuro, hay incluso una variedad que es negra / Hay un poco de verdadero, verdadero rojo aquí abajo / Valeriana roja original / Pero en la parte de arriba, se puede ver cuánto más llamativos son los rojos o el rojo cobrizo / Podemos ver un nuevo tono muy rojo ahí mismo / Algunos rojos más oscuros, no tan anaranjados / Con el color más rojo en la parte de atrás, y además esa flor / Por supuesto, toma ese tinte rojizo característico y se transforma en una hoja muy verde, éstas son muy verdes, pero empiezan así, incluso los tallos son rojos / Este aspecto cambiante de la hoja nueva aquí, con el rojo y el verde claro / Su tallo se ve rojo / Probablemente encontremos unos pocos lugares donde las hojas se han vuelto rojas; puedes ver cómo empiezan / Y a veces está completamente coronado de rojo / Las hojas, en éstos, se tornan realmente rojas. BLANCO: Tonos de blanco / Es un blanco aterciopelado / Un blanco salpicado de verde y gris / Sabes, cada uno de estos blancos claros / Es una flor blanca / Ésta se volverá casi completamente blanca con apenas manchas de verde / Blanco que juega con la luz / Algunas difíciles de distinguir, sin duda eclipsadas por el resplandor del blanco / Situadas en la parte superior del tallo entre blanco y gris / Pero lo llamamos blanco; le gusta mezclar un poquito de lavanda a veces, puedes ver esa pequeña flor / Y el blanco es un contraste realmente bonito con él / O los bordes blancos de un amarillo viejo / No hay nada que iguale la suavidad de este blanco / Pero es simplemente ese blanco inmaculado / A veces el blanco es el color más elegante / Blanco suave / A veces casi blanco durante el año, y tiene ese gris / Y expone este blanco / Es un cono blanco / Flotilla de blanco, blanco brillante / Blanco y rosa / La lantana blanca rastrera / Linda flor blanco brillante, ocasionalmente con pequeñas manchas de púrpura, los rosados florecientes / Capas de blanco y sombra, cada capa sombreando o matizando la siguiente capa / Algunas de ellas, al sol, adquieren casi un blanco. CREMA: Y crema / Crema y verde en el fondo / Crema y marrón, incluso verdes, matices de verde / Y un nuevo color crema / Incluso un pequeño borde crema; es un amarillo muy, muy alegre / Bonito color crema y amarillo y rosado. ANARANJADO: Tonos de anaranjado / Un naranja sobre verde alzándose hacia el cielo / Un naranja fuerte / De modo que tiene los anaranjados y los rojos que hemos observado en otro / Entonces, no sé cuán naranja o amarillo terminará / Apenas del otro lado del árbol, son de un color más anaranjado / Éste es el anaranjado, que no está haciendo nada en este momento / Y este otro es anaranjado / De algún modo disfruto de la visión de este reflejo del lado de atrás de este árbol naranja y amarillo / El anaranjado de la pata de canguro allá arriba / Tiene en ella el naranja y el amarillo / Cuando florece completamente puede ser toda anaranjada. AMARILLO Y ORO: Amarillo moteado de verde / Es la lantana amarilla / Campanillas amarillas / Atractivo amarillo con un toque de verde lima / Estos escurridizos amarillos pálidos y verdes claros, que apenas despiertan / Una confusión de amarillos y verdes salpicados de rojos y herrumbre / Que pronto serán amarillos / Y un poco de amarillo tierno / Amarillo vibrante que se combina con el sol y lo refleja, brillante y hermoso... (oh... imagina estar creando colores) bordeado de rojo / Amarillo sol / Un amarillo maduro, que se vuelve blanco / Risueño resplandor de amarillo y púrpura y lavanda, crema y verde en el fondo / Nuestra hierba de San Juan / Amarillo y rojo llamativos / Los dorados, y los verdes, y los amarillos / Un amarillo limón claro / Un alegre amarillo brillante con una especie de sonrisa de rojo y una flor amarilla y de un leve gris verdoso, incluso un pequeño borde crema / Un amarillo claro / Amarillo intenso / Este amarillento tenue / Amarillo radiante / Y una vez que se abre, aparece la floración amarilla / Aquí los colores, sabes, como están saliendo del ciclo invernal, son un poco amarillos, pero regresan a esto, nuevamente a una clase de muy / Pequeña flor amarilla [que] brotará / No puedes olvidar los amarillos vivos y luego este rojo intenso / Tenemos una especie de combinación de amarillo, naranja / Brillo ámbar / Ves, tal vez es una pizca de ámbar o va a convertirse en un color ámbar / Pero parecen medallones de oro que flotan sobre la planta / Tu vista pasea por ese amarillo vivo de ahí y te obliga a mirar / Es interesante, también, ver cuán amarillos pueden ser algunos de ellos / La diferencia de color en los amarillos / Observa qué distinto es en las áreas más sombreadas, qué intensos son los amarillos en las áreas más soleadas / Color amarillo vivo, llamativo, alegre en la parte de atrás / Algunas de las hojas más viejas tienen un amarillo más oscuro / Posiblemente un ámbar / No hay nada más fresco que un amarillo / Y brota este amarillo fuerte, intenso / Dos variedades diferentes de amarillo / Y solo amarillo / Un tipo de flor pequeña amarillenta, pero no puedes saberlo hasta que se abre, puedes ver el amarillo en torno de ella, pero parece como si pudiera ser incluso un púrpura / Amarillo; un poco / Y si miras detenidamente, tiene una garganta casi amarillenta / A veces me pregunto si no es un reflejo del verde / Afectadas por la intemperie, son un poco más amarillas, pero reverdecerán y se pondrán más erguidas / Pero no puedes evitar mirarlas, porque tienen esa pequeña mancha amarilla, que dice: estoy aquí / El amarillo oscuro, el jaspeado y el otro / Hay un color casi lima, crema. VERDE: Verde jaspeado, que cambia a / Verde brillante / Verde brillante e intenso / Verde brillante con un matiz de amarillo y rosa y crema / Los efectos claros y oscuros de los colores verde hierba / Verdes jaspeados y blanco cremoso, verde oscuro, verde claro / Verde oscuro, brillante / Los verdes iluminados por el sol y los verdes sombreados / Un tono de verde único, que envuelve a las que pronto serán flores / Verdes brillantes, resplandecientes, manchas y pintas caóticas de verde y crema / Una colaboración de verde con rojo y púrpura y amarillo / Verde reluciente, brillante y mate / Matices de verde, claro, oscuro que pasa gradualmente al marrón / Un verde musgoso / Líneas verdes, que parecen un río que corre, un río de verde / Compartiendo con el verde, compartiendo el verde con el rojo y el púrpura / Y verde y gris y verde grisáceo / Verde helecho... con un verde amarillento más claro / Que abraza los verdes y amarillos y púrpuras y lavanda a su alrededor / El brote más antiguo del verde teñido con rojo o ámbar / Rodeado por tonos de verde / Austero verde pálido / Verde claro, verde oscuro / Hojas de un verde intermedio con una parte inferior gris / Es verde, rosado, rojo, púrpura / Y a veces es simplemente verde, casi / El brote nuevo en los verdes, rosados y púrpuras / Una parte superior verde grisáceo o incluso verde más oscuro, y una inferior parecida al verde fieltro, tallos de aspecto suave / Tallos verdes, y rojo / El color que llamo *chartreuse* [verde amarillento] / Un futuro de *chartreuse*, lima, un tipo de verde lima / Hermoso verde oscuro y verde claro / Matices de verde oscuro / Verde suave y claro / Verde más oscuro arriba, pero en realidad solo un verde medio / Verdes grisáceos y vetas amarillas / Y ésta tiene una pequeña hoja verde muy cálida / Sabes, te va a provocar con una hoja de un verde realmente oscuro también / Verde grisáceo abajo y, a la distancia, verás mucho gris verdoso / Donde tienes una multitud de verdes / También puedes tener ese verde brillante resplandeciente / Y siempre tiene una pizca de un tipo de verde lima o amarillo / No hay un nombre verdaderamente adecuado para ese verde, está entre un verde grisáceo y un verde casi azulado / Esta variedad tiene un verde un poquito más claro en la hoja, y un blanco / Está casi como salpicada de verde / Solo verde oscuro y muy exuberante / Verde y fuerte / Con ese bonito verde / Este gran tronco verde / Filtra tu vista cuando miras cosas muy verdes, y da al jardín un aspecto verdaderamente colorido / Es casi una sombra de color sobre el verde / Éste es principalmente verde, un poco de color alrededor de lo austero / La parte inferior verde aquí / Y durante un tiempo, incluso, es un tipo de verde delicado y de apariencia suave / Y luego esto aflora de estas cubiertas verdes / Éste tiene un verde más claro, mucho más claro, también / Pero está cambiando, y una parte está volviendo a ese verde original / Y aún verdean / Mira este verde oscuro allí abajo / Muy nuevo, muy verde / Las hojas son casi de un verde lima alrededor del verde, en contraste con ese amarillo, y se están volviendo verdes / Y tienes esas pocas que simplemente se niegan a tornarse verdes y permanecen amarillas / De modo que es mayormente verde, y luego... ¡bum! / Una especie de verde básico, y bueno para sombra / Un manto de flores sobre esta planta verde / Estas hojas son mucho más verdes, estas hojas bajas tienen un hermoso verde oscuro y brillante / Así que tendrás más verde, pero menos flores / A veces me pregunto si es un reflejo del verde / Hoja más grande, menos verde / Aquí nuevamente ves qué bonitas y verdes son éstas, y cuelgan en el área sombreada / Pero es una especie de verde amarillento / Más claro que ese verde oscuro cuando maduran /

Veinte colores diferentes de verde / Cincuenta matices de verde / Los varios matices de verde arriba / Verde si lo tomas de este modo, púrpura si lo tomas así / ¿Es un tallo verde o es un tallo anaranjado? Todo verde hasta aquí, y aquí está apareciendo la flor, y puedes ver el naranja en su garganta, aquí en el cuello. Verde seco. AZUL: El azul salpicado de blanco / Que pronto se convertirá en este azul / Matices de azul / El azul y el blanco brillante pero delicado / Estas minúsculas flores azules y amarillas / Ésta se llama dianela azul, y también tiene esa flor azul / Pero se destaca claramente entre los azules / La llamamos azul porque tiene un toque azul en la flor de tipo verde azulado y púrpura, con un poco de blanco / Y se ve bien con los azules y los púrpuras y los blancos / Ésta tiene una espiga azul, es una salvia azul / Espigas azul oscuro, muy atractivas a la vista / Las flores del cielo, como se las llama, se derraman del árbol / Es increíble, es casi un añil / Es el azul más intenso, también con este tipo de hoja verde amarillento / Un azul que es casi imposible / Y cuando crece te engaña y toma ese color añil / Sabes, casi una clase de azul fluorescente / Aquí no tienes los azules y púrpuras y los centros amarillos, los tallos tienen rojo / Sabes, todas las versiones de la flor del cielo son azules. VIOLETA: Es una dama del monte / Espiga púrpura / Pétalos lavanda / Espigas de púrpura y azul / Un púrpura brillante / Lavanda, crema y amarillo, con un matiz púrpura en las puntas / Con vetas de un púrpura muy claro, tal vez rojo / El color inicial púrpura y verde / El brote púrpura y verde y rojo y herrumbre / Una combinación casi inconcebible de púrpura y verde... y verde, y verde y púrpura, claro y aterciopelado / El atractivo lavanda / El lavanda de la lavanda / Púrpura muy oscuro / Con un púrpura más claro / Casi lavanda, como la lavanda / Minúsculas flores púrpura oscuro / Lavanda y un gris / Si miras el lado púrpura y el lado verde del brote nuevo / Púrpura arremolinado del brote nuevo / Con su borde parecido al cabello... púrpuras, rojos / Pequeña flor púrpura, parece tan tímida / Una espiga de púrpuras y blancos / Hubo un llamado de alerta para el despertar de las espigas púrpura / Un púrpura tan, tan oscuro al principio / Púrpura o azul o púrpura y blanco, azul y blanco / ¿O color lavanda de mar? / O uno la mira y piensa:

ésta va a ser una flor púrpura / Empieza con estos bordes púrpura / Tenemos estos púrpuras / Flor de lavanda / Una especie de color púrpura / Cuando uno las mira más detenidamente, los púrpuras se decoloran como si se los hubiera pintado con acuarela / El lavanda más oscuro aquí, y luego se decolora hacia el centro de cada uno de los pétalos / Y se convierte en una especie de color malva / De púrpura muy, muy oscuro, cambia a colores anaranjados y aherrumbrados / Cuando el blanco surge del púrpura / El brote nuevo tiene ese aspecto casi púrpura y luego se vuelve verde, pero no siempre / Una bonita mezcla de púrpura y verde y una flor que parece vellosa / A medida que crece, se puede ver que el púrpura es el brote nuevo / Y algunos de ellos permanecerán púrpura, y algunos se volverán de un verde muy oscuro, pero es algo así como un verde apagado, no es realmente una planta brillante / Pero es como una combinación de esta delicada flor de una especie de rosa lavanda y una hoja un poco más rígida / Una flor purpúrea verdaderamente bonita / Y ésta está comenzando a perder ese púrpura / Hojas pequeñas, púrpura oscuro / Y puedes ver cómo los tonos de lavanda... cambian / Pero ese púrpura oscuro, sabes, y aquí se aclara / Y es un púrpura muy, muy oscuro / Lavanda azulada, sartas de flores que se derraman / Y eso... abajo, tengo que llamarlo simplemente púrpura / Ves ese púrpura. ROSADO: Un fucsia vibrante, vibrante / Rosados sutiles y verdes apagados / Vetas de color rosado y púrpura / Fucsia translúcido o rojo / Un poco de rosado suave aquí / Y es un color realmente especial, es un fucsia / Y éste es el rosado / Es una flor muy agradable, muy rosada, de aspecto muy femenino / Realmente atrae la luz y el rosado se destaca, una planta verdaderamente hermosa / Tomará algo de color rosado y algo de amarillo y de rojizo, pero finalmente se vuelve muy blanca / Sabes, un rosado muy, muy claro / Habrá un par de flores que tengan ese rosado en todas las hojas / Y también tenemos algunas rosadas que aún no se han abierto / Se ve como un color fucsia un poco apagado, y luego aparece de pronto esta hermosa flor. GRIS Y PLATA: El efecto gris claro, casi blanco del lado de abajo de estas hojas / El gris claro con casi un blanco a la luz del sol, con un gris verdoso mezclado en él / Gris en los bordes / Gris y marrón que levanta el color / Gris claro, que se percibe como una textura / Gris / Un gris / Un estricto gris seco envuelto en crema / El gris y púrpura más oscuro de esta lavanda / El color gris verdoso apagado de los tallos / El gris y verde y púrpura / Este gris tiene un aspecto un poco sucio / Una apariencia grisácea, pero el gris es diferente / Una especie de gris, el verde arriba y el gris / Comparado con las hojas más viejas, se vuelve un gris realmente interesante / Ves el brote más viejo en el tronco, el gris, con un aspecto amarronado / Pero hay más grises que otra cosa en los troncos / Lavanda, es un gris lavanda / Éste es un gris o gris verdoso, sí / Y este otro, aquí, es más gris. NEGRO: Ésta, en particular, se llama caballero negro / Anillos perfectos de negro, amarillo y blanco / Si la miras, en cierto modo, hay... es casi negra... y, cuando crece, se burla de ti y adopta ese color añil / Con bordes negros. MARRÓN, HERRUMBRE, COBRE: El cobre y el púrpura / El sutil color herrumbre, las hojas de sutil color herrumbre contra las hojas púrpura / Hebras de marrón y verde que se expanden, entrelazadas con verde brillante muy oscuro y amarillo / Aunque marrones con el paso del tiempo / Marrón marchito rodeado de verde / Una corteza marrón realmente sólida / Marrones y grises / Parece como que muda a ciertos marrones y rojos y verdes, esta planta tiene mucho color, mucha vida... realmente se hace notar, realmente capta la luz / Allí, una especie de color herrumbre, creo / Hay una pizca de marrón ahí / La parte inferior de la corteza es muy marrón, y la coloreará durante un tiempo / Siempre espero que un árbol parezca... ¡marrón![43]

43 Shea en conversación con Meyenberg.

El jardín estaba distinto, menos cuidado. El sol seguía allí, no cabe duda, y la luz cubría el abandono de forma provisional. C. había dejado de cultivar las plantas que quería, porque no conseguía acordarse exactamente de sus nombres. Le dejaba al azar la selección de las especies. Conservaba en su memoria las manchas de color y su repetición temporal formando diferentes gamas. No podía deshacerse de esta estructura que le permitía seguir vivo. El jardín estaba lleno de circunloquios, cosa nada común [en el jardín y en C.]. Había perdido la iniciativa y no parecía interesado en entablar una conversación. Su vocabulario se tornó ininteligible, y el jardín, irreconocible. ¿Hay forma de que un jardín no se pueda leer? Si no hubiera sido por el recuerdo de las conversaciones pasadas, o por aquellos años previos a nuestro primer encuentro, probablemente yo no habría entendido nada. Ése es el problema cuando la comunicación es con palabras.

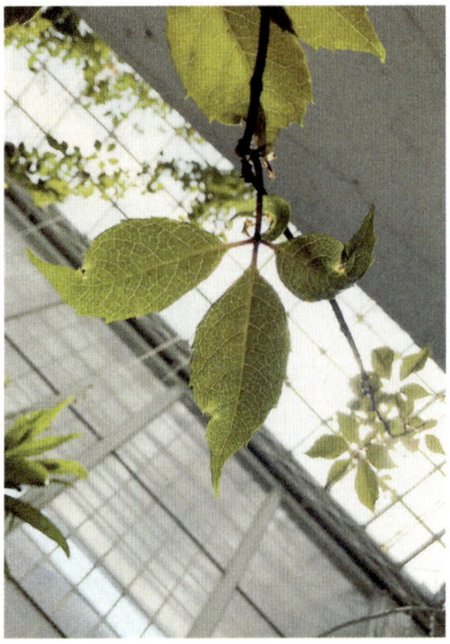

Me imagino que, en realidad, C. no estaba allí desde hacía tiempo. Ahora bien, si se había ido físicamente el jardín seguía existiendo por inercia. O tal vez los dos estaban allí y era yo quien se encontraba en aquella estación de la que hablaba el filósofo ateniense Albucius [y a la que tantas veces había hecho alusión C.]: la quinta estación, aquella en donde las esponjas se rompen [...] un residuo atemporal, un espejismo de la mente que, sin embargo, parece permanente ahora. Un lugar que no es distópico, ni utópico. El lugar donde se reformula el lenguaje antes de ser dicho.[44]

Se resiste a ser descrita.

44 Quignard, *op. cit.*, 57.

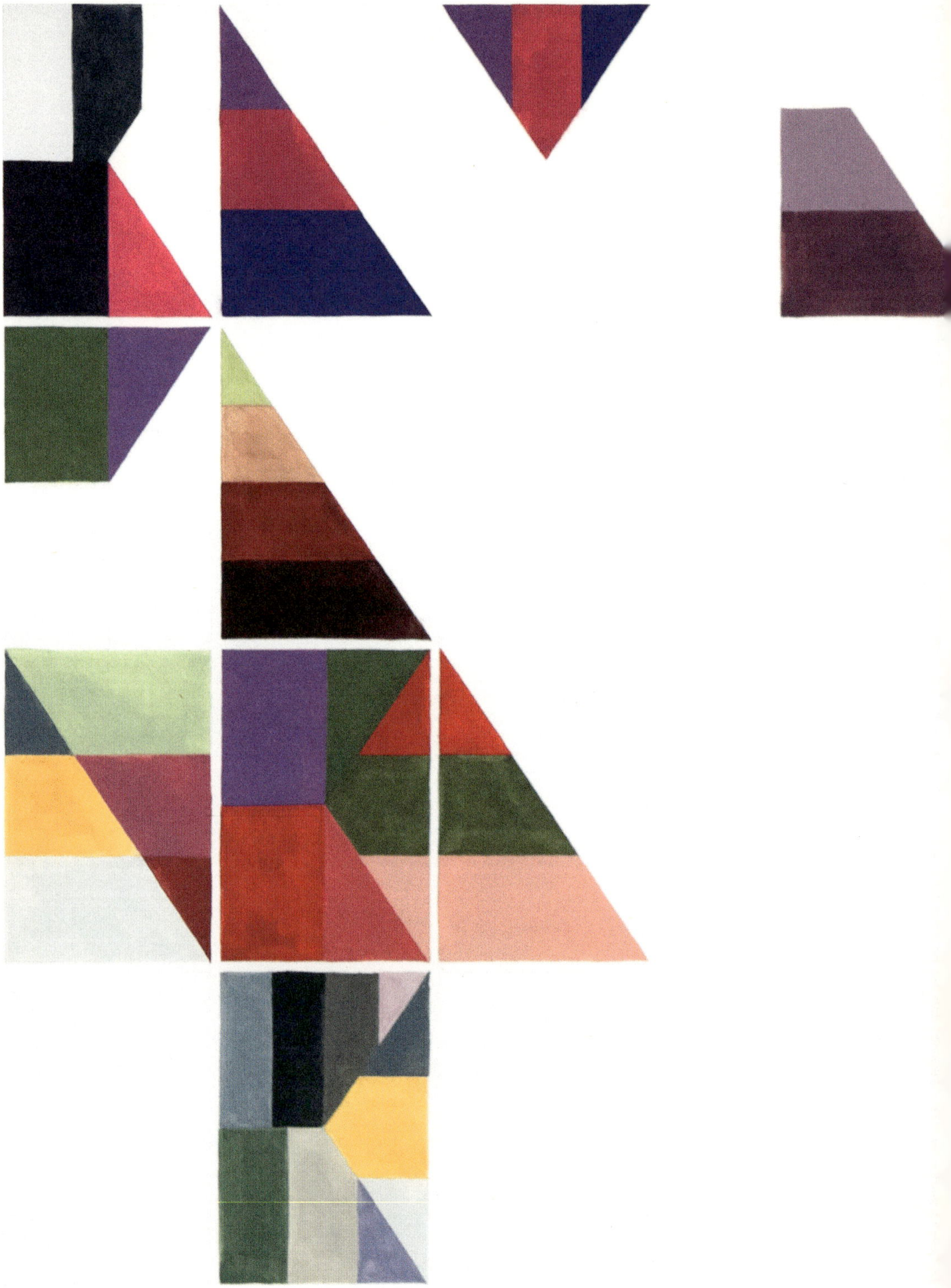

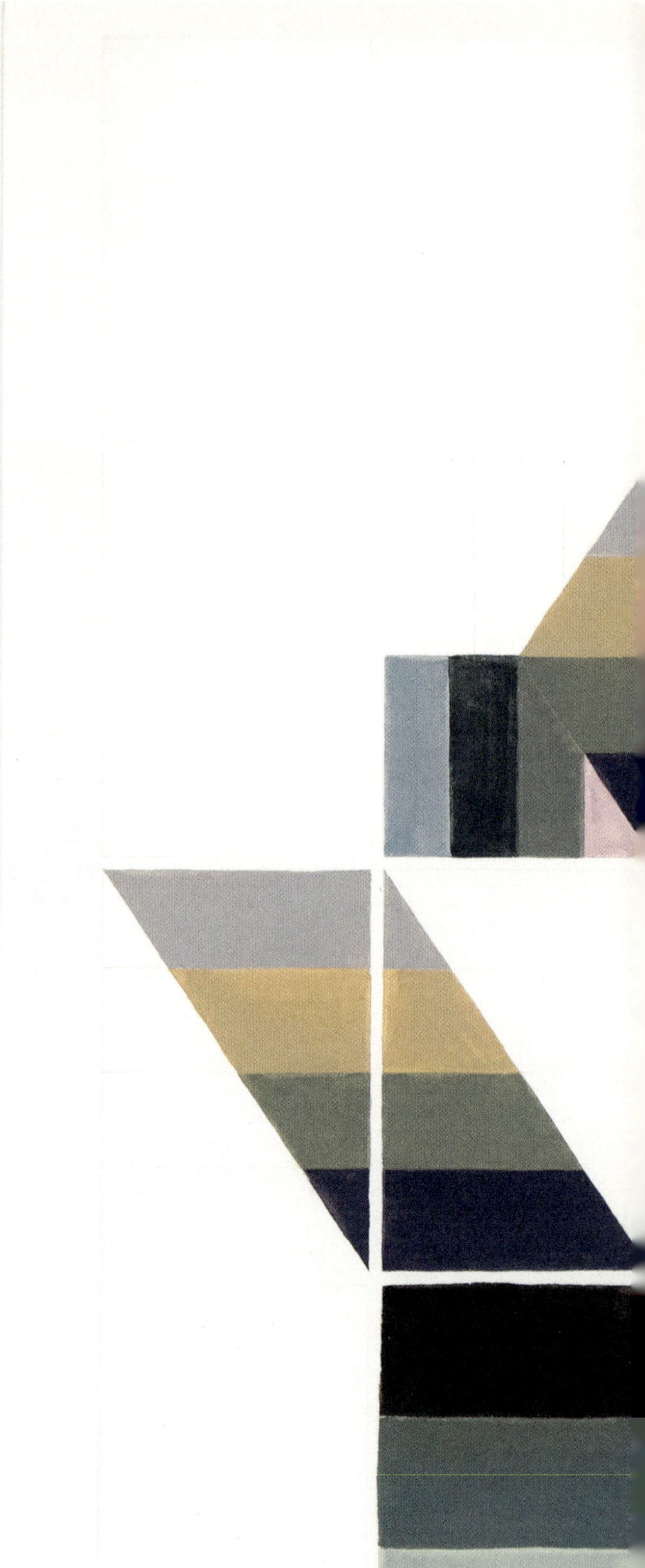

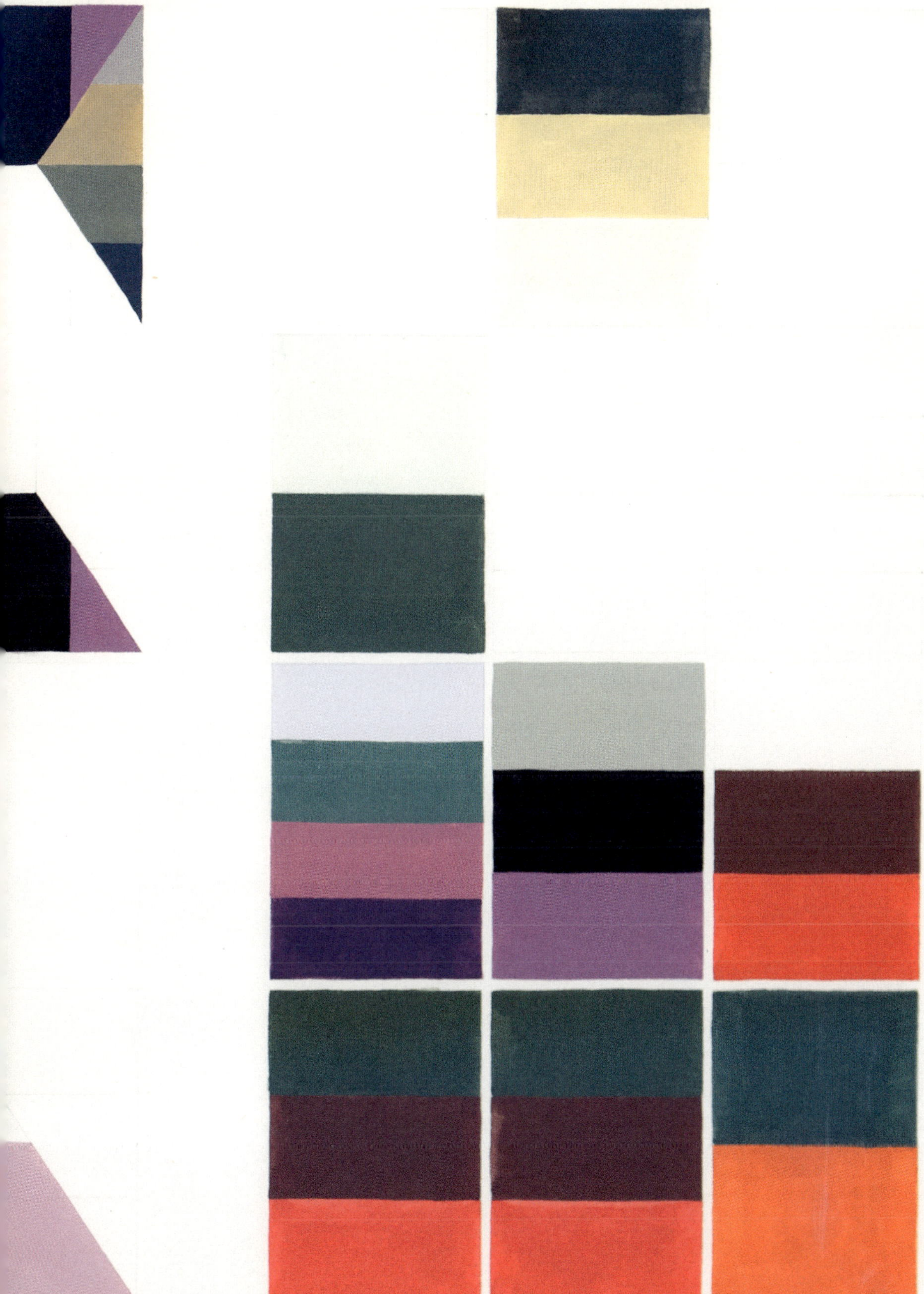

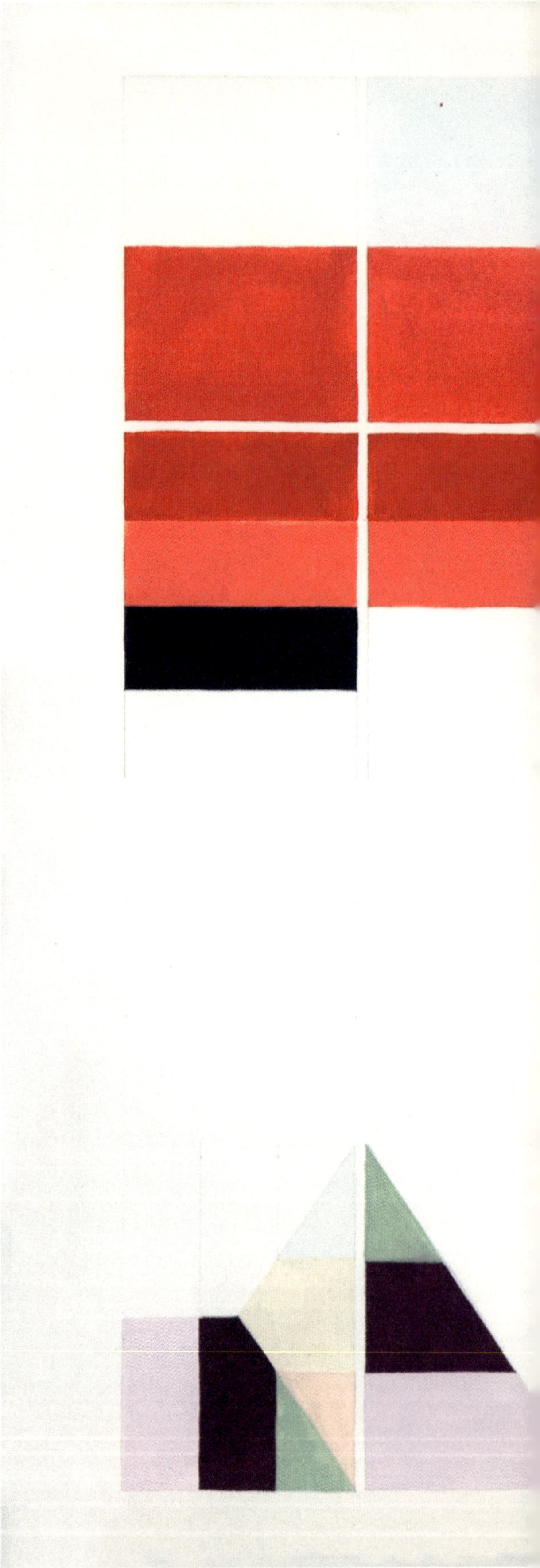

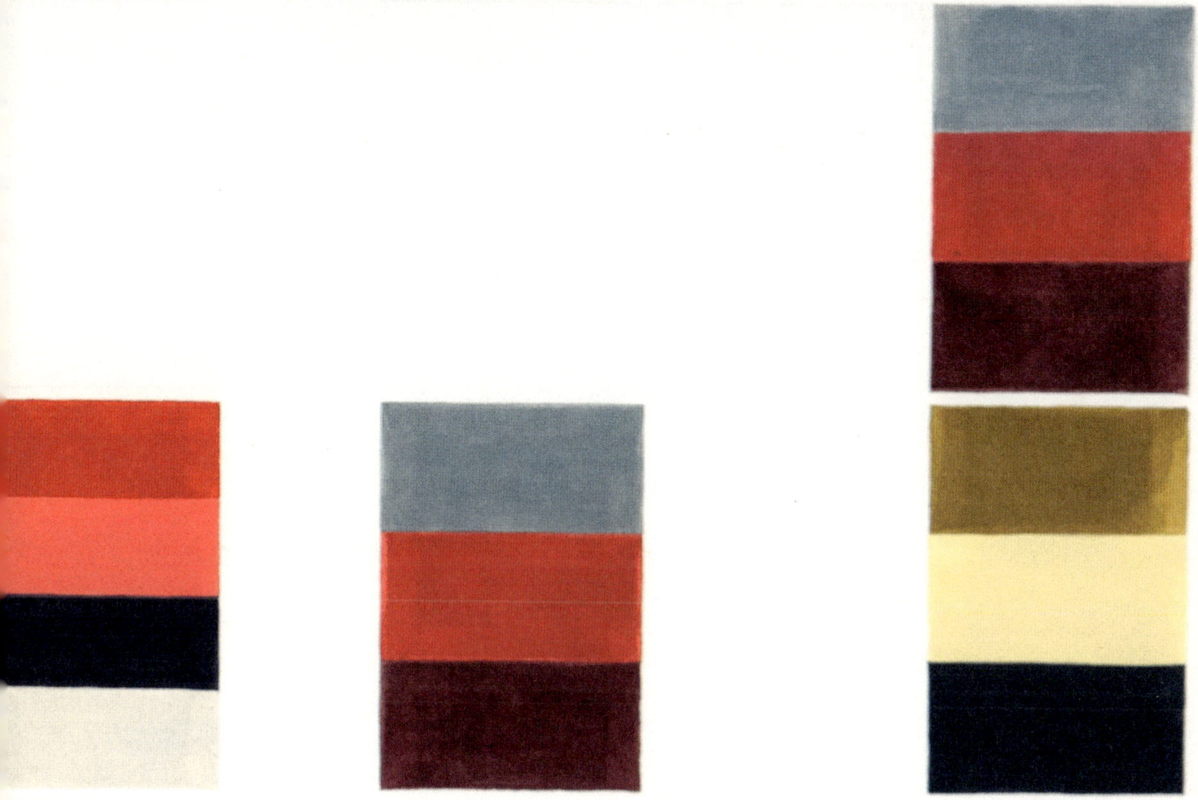

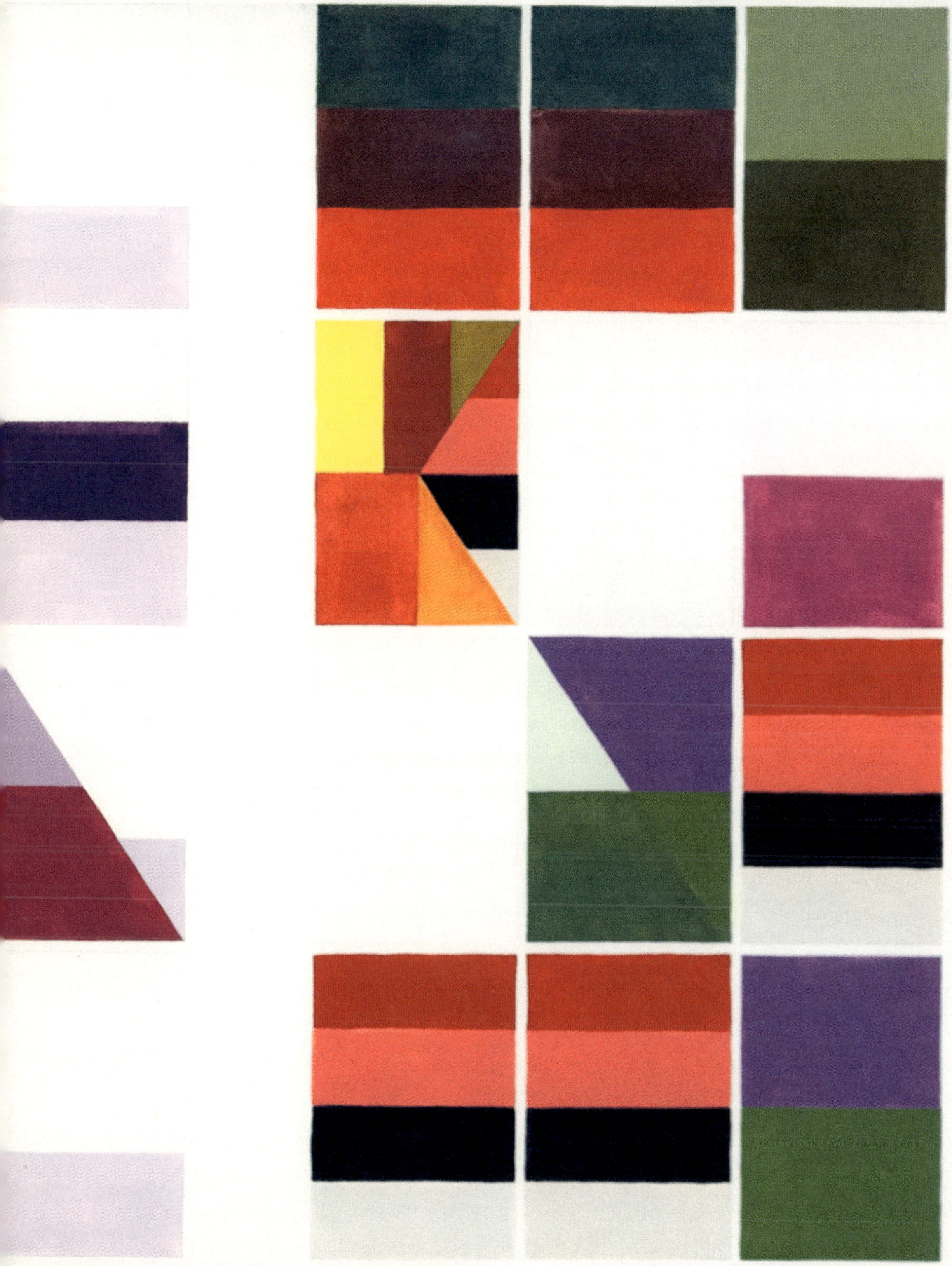

1.
Even When Fall Is Here (score), 2017
45 graphite-and-gouache paintings on 300 g. cotton paper
16 ½ x 14 ½ in. (41.9 x 36.9 cm) each
Collection of Eloisa Haudenschild

Even When Fall Is Here takes as its starting point a notebook composed by landscape designer Chris Shea over a period of two years. After he was diagnosed with a terminal illness, Shea prepared this book as an instruction manual for Eloisa Haudenschild, to help her identify and tend to the different plants, trees, bushes, and flowers grown in her garden once it was no longer under his care. Shea's notebook contained technical information about the plants as well as scientific, common, and even imaginary names he had given to certain species. It also included family pictures and personal information.

In Shea's notebook, Meyenberg found many photographs that were particularly evocative and personal, beyond mere documentation of the garden. He asked the gardener to take pictures of the eighty species in the garden again, this time focusing on the lighting, composition, and other specific details. Shea, with no formal training as a photographer, gave his imagination free reign, experimenting with different lenses to produce a portrait of the garden from his unique point of view.

As Meyenberg received Shea's pictures, he cataloged the eighty species again, assigning each a number according to the order in which they appear in the notebook.

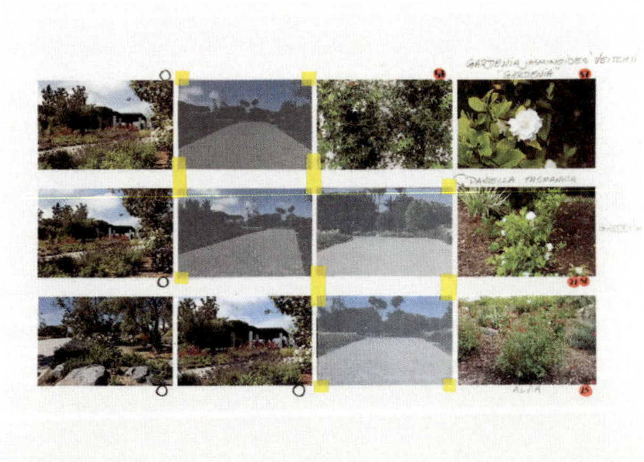

Chris Shea´s notebook, 2016-2018

Diario de Chris Sea, 2016-2018

1.

Even When Fall Is Here (score), 2017

45 pinturas hechas con grafito y gouache en papel algodón de 300 g.

16 ½ x 14 ½ in. (41,9 x 36,9 cm) cada una

Colección de Eloisa Haudenschild

Even When Fall Is Here tiene como punto de partida un diario elaborado por el diseñador de paisajes Chris Shea durante el transcurso de dos años. Después de que se le diagnosticara una enfermedad terminal, Shea preparó este libro como un manual para ayudar a Eloisa Haudenschild con el reconocimiento de las diferentes plantas, árboles, arbustos y flores que habían sembrado en el jardín, una vez que él ya no estuviera a cargo de éste. La bitácora contenía datos técnicos sobre las plantas, nombres científicos, comunes y nombres imaginarios con los que habían rebautizado algunas especies. El cuaderno incluía también fotos familiares y datos personales.

Meyenberg encontró en este documento varias fotografías que le parecieron especialmente sensibles y personales y que iban más allá de la simple documentación del jardín, ya sea por el momento de luz del día, el encuadre, o algún detalle concreto.

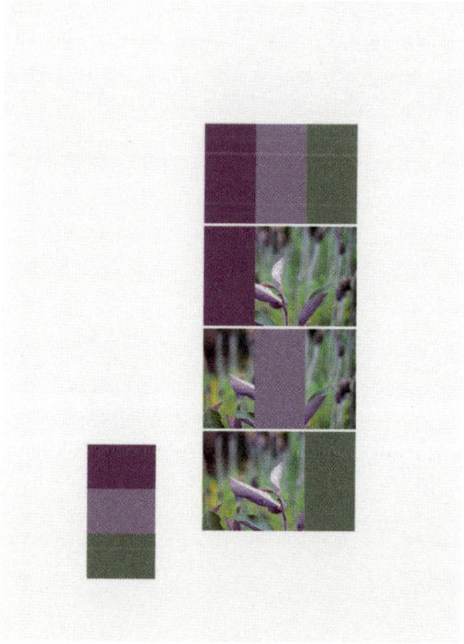

Color coded image, 2017

Imagen de un código de color, 2017

After careful examination of the images, Meyenberg color coded all of the pictures according to the dominant colors of each group of plants. When two colors were dominant, he divided the pictures in half with two symmetrical color areas. With more complex compositions, he split the pictures into thirds and assigned three corresponding blocks of color. He divided the most chromatically complex pictures into four color sections.

The next step was to replace the pictures from Shea's notebook with these color-coded images. In the notebook, each page, roughly tabloid size, contained twelve photos: three rows of four photos each. Meyenberg replicated this scale and twelve-grid arrangement in his resulting suite of forty-five paintings.

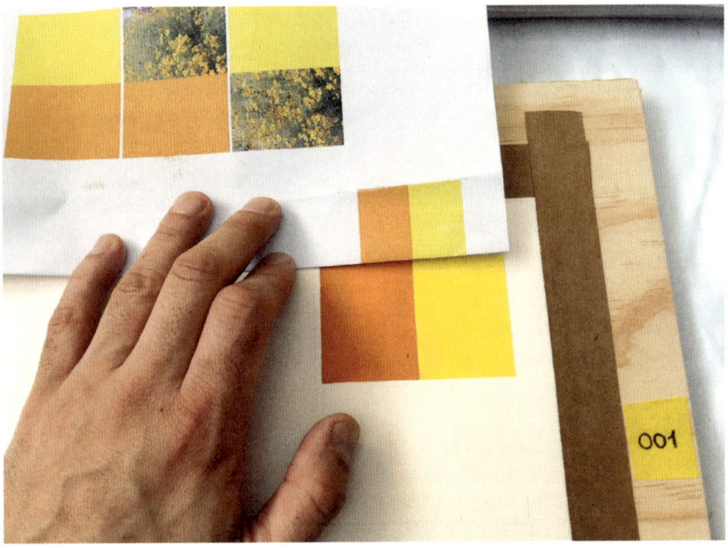

Color coded image (detail). Erick Meyenberg´s atelier in Mexico City, 2017

Códigos de color (detalle). Estudio de Erick Meyenberg en Ciudad de México, 2017

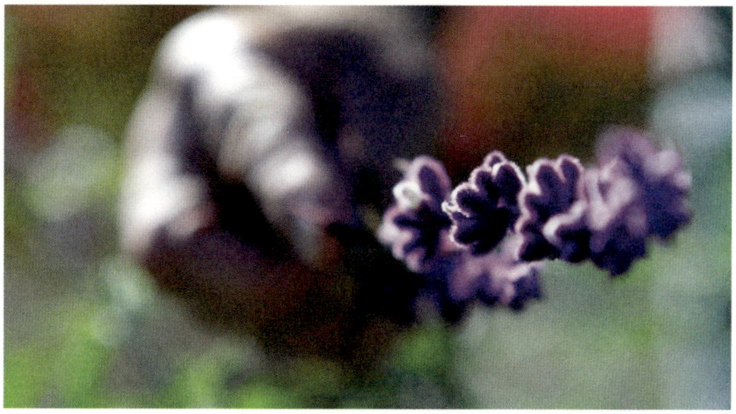

Even When Fall Is Here, 2018
Video still

Even When Fall Is Here, 2018
Still de video

Después de dialogar con Eloisa y Chris, Meyenberg le pidió al jardinero que volviera a fotografiar las ochenta especies del jardín, pero deteniéndose en la iluminación, la composición, y otros específicos detalles. Shea, el cual nunca se había dedicado a la fotografía, decidió dar rienda suelta a su imaginación y experimentar con diferentes lentes para establecer un retrato del jardín desde un punto de vista nuevo y sensible.

Según iba recibiendo las fotografías de Shea, Meyenberg catalogó nuevamente las ochenta especies con un número, siguiendo el orden de aparición en la bitácora.

Después de un cuidadoso análisis de las imágenes, hizo la conversión de todas las fotografías a una codificación cromática, siguiendo los colores dominantes de cada grupo de plantas. Cuando dos colores eran dominantes, dividió la imagen en dos áreas simétricas. Con construcciones más complejas, separaba las imágenes en tres, asignando sus correspondientes bloques de color. Así hasta un máximo de cuatro franjas de color.

El siguiente paso fue sustituir las fotografías de la bitácora de Chris Shea por estos códigos de color. La bitácora estaba hecha de la siguiente manera: cada hoja, aproximadamente tamaño doble carta, en posición horizontal, constaba de doce fotografías: tres filas con cuatro fotografías.

He began by creating a color chart for each plant species, replicating as closely as possible the digital colors by hand in gouache on a series of cards. Each card includes a written formula and records the trials and errors in matching the hues.

He left blank spaces in the grid, and in some sections, the geometric color blocks are incomplete. In this way, the paintings replicate the rhythm of the garden and its natural cycles.

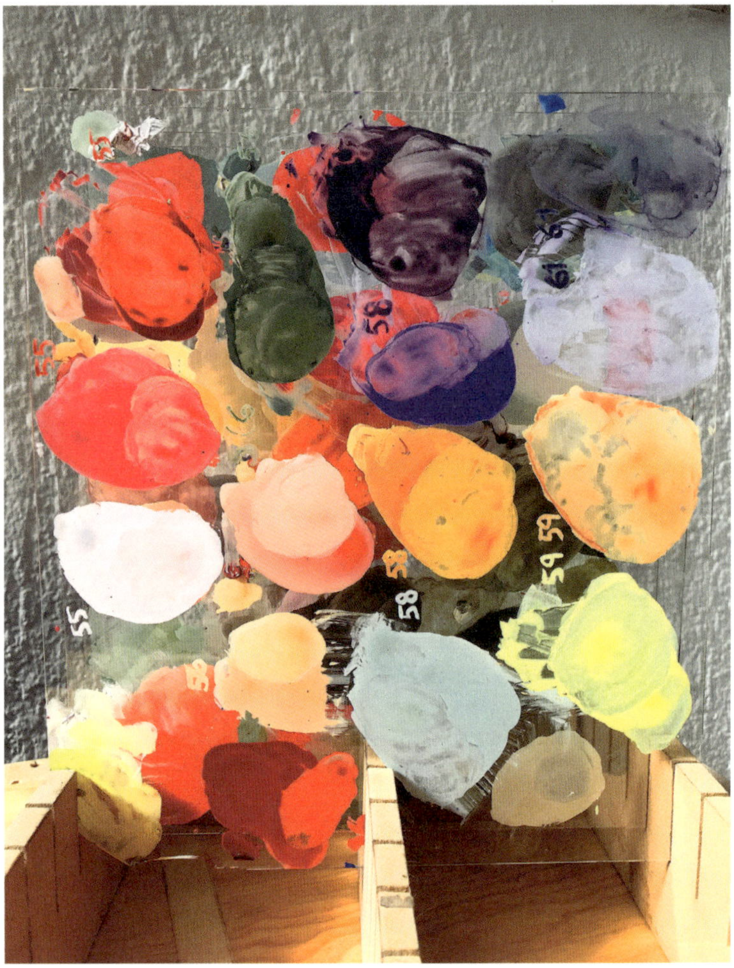

Color palette on glass (detail)

Paleta de color en cristal (detalle)

Meyenberg replicó esta escala en una retícula de doce cuadrantes, resultando una composición total de cuarenta y cinco pinturas.

Empezó realizando una gama de color para cada especie de planta, replicando los colores digitales a mano, en gouache, en una serie de tarjetas. Cada tarjeta incluía una fórmula escrita y reproducía las pruebas y los errores en la combinación de tonalidades.

Meyenberg dejó espacio en blanco dentro de la cuadrícula, y en algunas secciones los bloques quedan incompletos. Así, las pinturas replican el ritmo del jardín y sus ciclos naturales.

Even When Fall Is Here, 2017

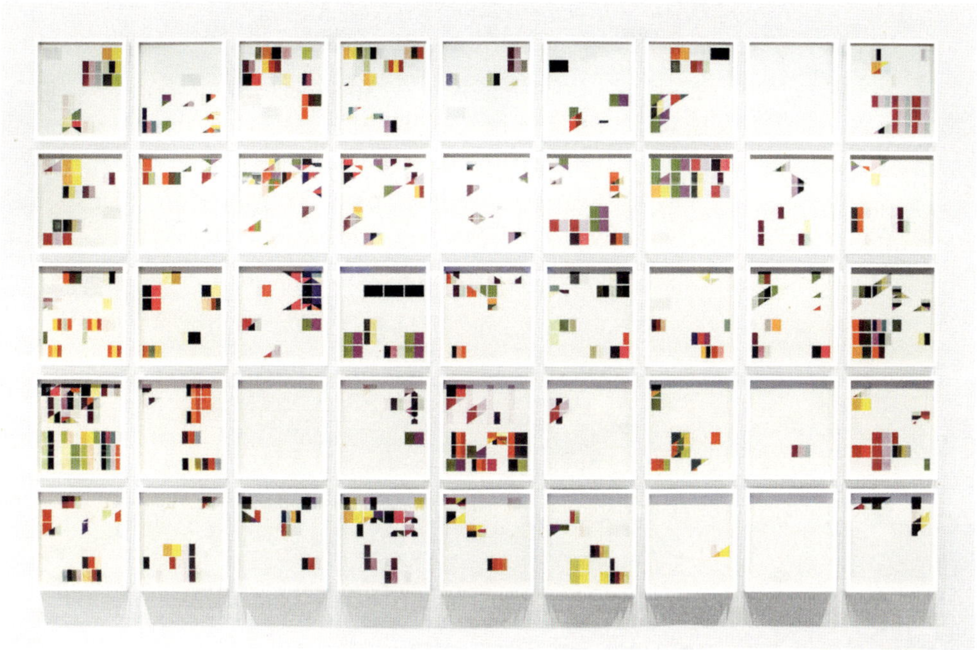

2.
Even When Fall Is Here, 2018
Six-channel video installation, color, sound
20:22 minutes
Martha UC: video editing
Natalia Pérez Turner: cello improvisation
Martin de Torcy: sound design
Félix Blume: sound design advisor
Collection of Eloisa Haudenschild

During Meyenberg's visits to the garden, he took video footage of Shea's hands touching the plants. As time went by, Meyenberg also began to record conversations with the gardener, who, little by little, opened up to him. Most of the discussions between the two men related to color and how Shea used it to describe the garden objectively. They also talked about Shea's life and proximity to death, given the fact of his illness.

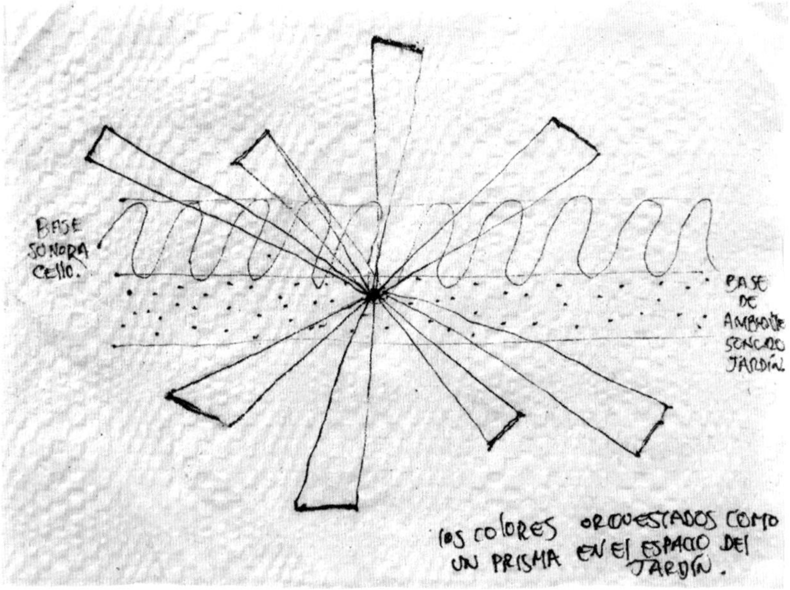

Sketch for the video installation (*Even When Fall Is Here*), 2018

Boceto para la instalación de video (*Even When Fall Is Here*), 2018

From these recordings, Meyenberg created a six-channel video installation with each channel representing a different color in the spectrum. He installed the videos in Haudenschild's garden in a semi-circle, as if they were a chorus. In the audio, not only can we hear Shea's voice and his footsteps, but also the sounds of the garden: birds, insects, the wind. Meyenberg also included the sound of a cello, the musical instrument that, according to Shea, most closely resembles the timbre of a human voice.

2.
Even When Fall Is Here, 2018
Video en seis canales, color y sonido
20:22 minutos
Martha UC: edición del video
Natalia Pérez Turner: improvisación con el cello
Martin de Torcy: diseño de sonido
Félix Blume: consejero de sonido
Colección de Eloisa Haudenschild

Durante las visitas al jardín, Meyenberg solía filmar las manos de Shea tocando las plantas. Según pasaba el tiempo, también empezó a grabar las conversaciones con el jardinero, quien lentamente comenzó a abrirse con él. La mayor parte de sus conversaciones remitían al color y a las descripciones precisas que Shea hacía del jardín. También solían hablar de la vida de ambos y la proximidad con la muerte que Shea tenía, dada su enfermedad.

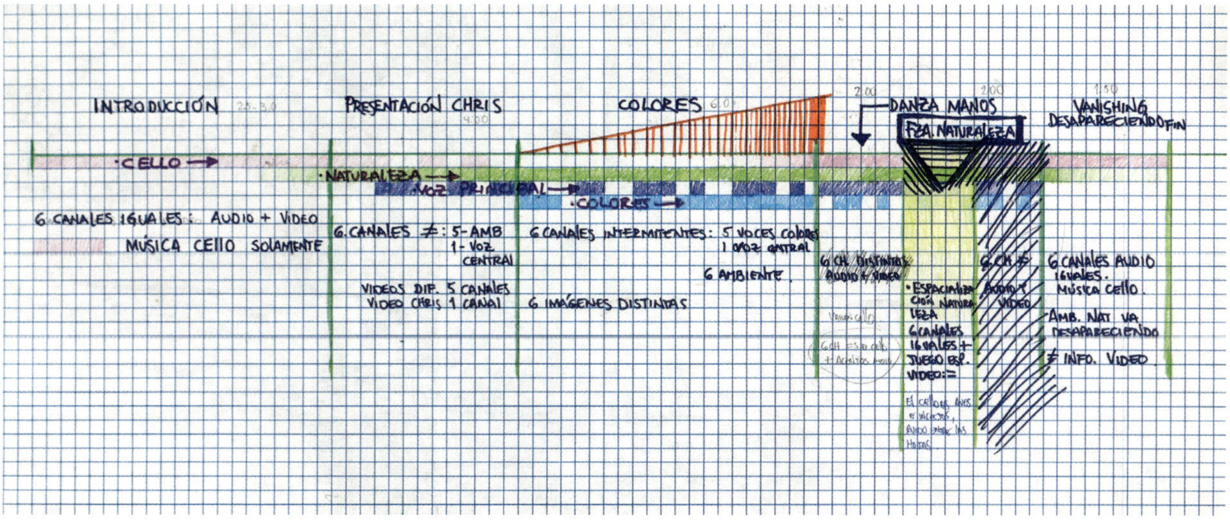

Sketch for the video installation (*Even When Fall Is Here*), 2018

Boceto para la instalación de video (*Even When Fall Is Here*), 2018

De estas grabaciones, Meyenberg creó una videoinstalación en seis canales, en la que cada canal representa un color diferente del espectro. Los videos se instalaron en el jardín de Haudenschild formando un semicírculo, como si fuera un coro. En este audio se pueden escuchar la voz y los pasos de Shea, pero también los sonidos del jardín: los pájaros, los insectos y el viento. Meyenberg también incluyó la melodía de un cello, por ser el instrumento musical que, según él, más se acerca al timbre de la voz humana.

The music was composed by Natalia Pérez Turner, a cellist devoted to contemporary music and improvisation. From Meyenberg's accounts of the garden and Shea's recordings, Pérez Turner created improvised melodies. These cello pieces accompany Shea's voice and the ambient garden sounds recorded by Meyenberg on their walks.

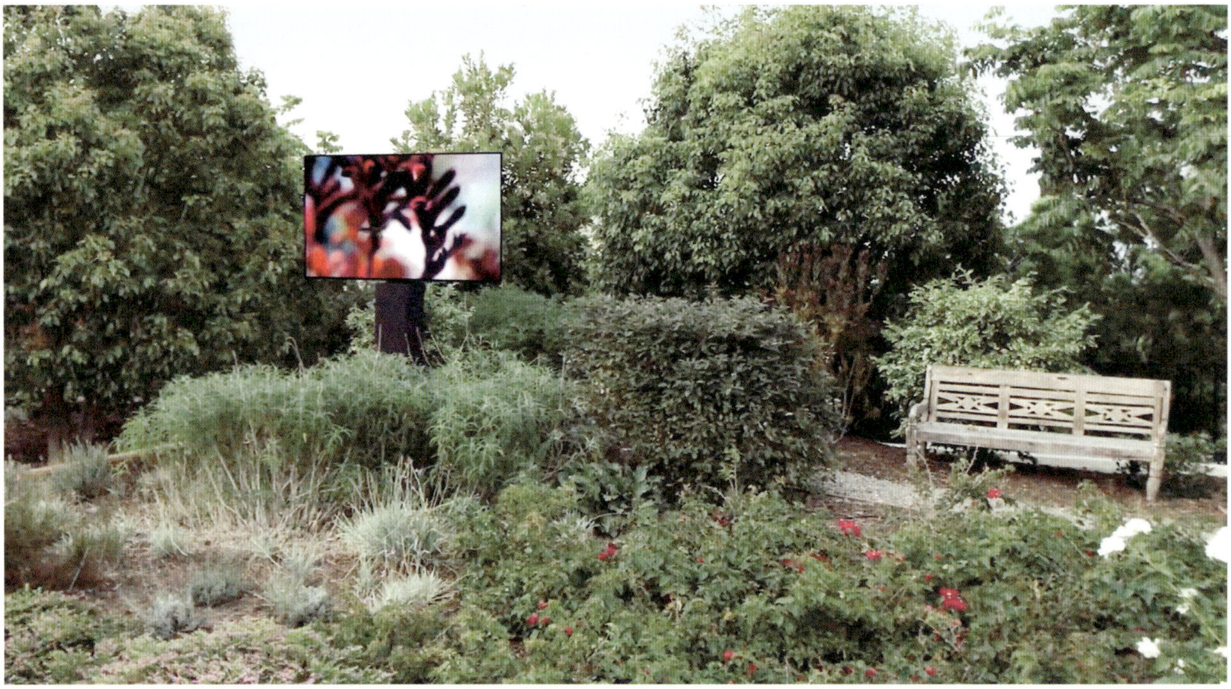

La música fue compuesta por Natalia Pérez Turner, una celista especializada en música contemporánea e improvisación. De las imágenes de Meyenberg y las grabaciones de Shea en el jardín, Pérez Turner creó melodías improvisadas que acompañaron la voz de Shea y el ambiente del jardín durante sus caminatas.

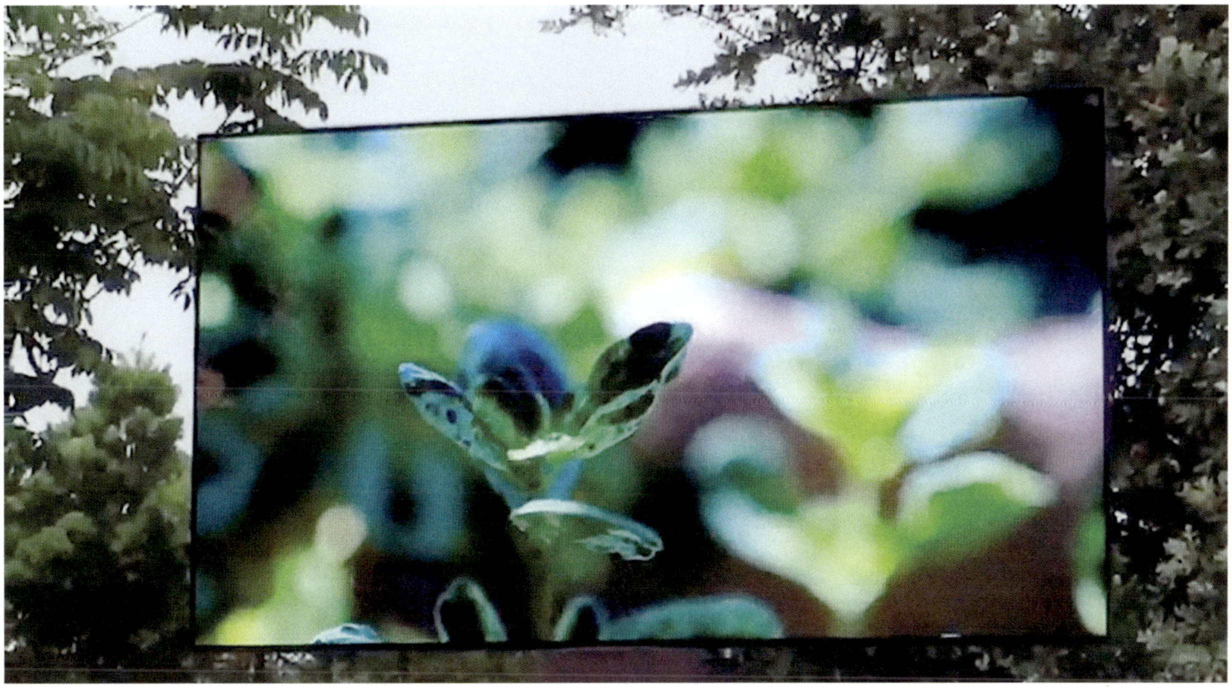

Even When Fall Is Here, 2018
Video installation at the garden of *haudenschild*Garage (detail). Photo by Erick Meyenberg

Even When Fall Is Here, 2018
Videoinstalación en el *haudenschild*Garage (detalle). Foto de Erick Meyenberg

Erick Meyenberg (Mexico City, 1980) is a Mexico City-based artist. He holds an MFA from the Berlin University of the Arts (UdK) in Germany and a BA in Visual Arts from the National School of Fine Arts (ENAP-UNAM) in Mexico. His work has been included in solo and group exhibitions in Mexico, Germany, Austria, Spain, Canada, the United States, the United Kingdom, and Japan and in the public collections of the Amparo Museum, Puebla, Mexico; Museum of Contemporary Art-UNAM (MUAC), Mexico City; The Benetton Foundation, Milan and Rome, Italy; and Telefónica Foundation, Mexico.

Ruth Estévez is a curator and writer based in Mexico City and Boston. She is senior curator-at-large at The Rose Art Museum in Boston and co-curator of the 34th São Paolo Biennial. She is the 2019 co-curator of *Idiorhythmias*, an annual program of performance, music, poetry, and text at the Barcelona Museum of Contemporary Art (MACBA). Estévez was director and curator at the Gallery at Roy and Edna Disney/CalArts Theater (REDCAT) in Los Angeles from 2012 to 2018 and chief curator at the Carrillo Gil Art Museum in Mexico City from 2007 to 2012. In 2010, Estévez founded LIGA-Space for Architecture, a nonprofit platform focused on experimentation in architecture, urbanism, and public art.

*haudenschild*Garage

Founded in 2003 by Eloisa Haudenschild, the *haudenschild*Garage seeks to provide cultural platforms through which international and regional artists are encouraged to experiment and engage in broad-ranging dialogues. The goal is to offer a facilitative context for opinion and production. The *haudenschild*Garage collaborates directly with artists through Projects and Commissions, Garage Talks, Fuel4Talks and Artist Residencies.

Erick Meyenberg (Ciudad de México, 1980) es un artista que vive en Ciudad de México. Tiene una maestría por la Berlin University of the Arts (UdK), Alemania, y una licenciatura en Artes Visuales por la Escuela Nacional de Artes Plásticas (ENAP-UNAM) de México. Su trabajo ha sido incluido en exposiciones individuales y grupales en México, Alemania, Austria, España, Canadá, Estados Unidos, Inglaterra y Japón. Su obra está en colecciones públicas como el Museo Amparo, Puebla; el Museo Universitario de Arte Contemporáneo de la UNAM (MUAC), Ciudad de México; The Benetton Foundation, Milán y Roma; y la Fundación Telefónica, México.

Ruth Estévez es una curadora y escritora basada en Ciudad de México y Boston. Es curadora sénior del Rose Art Museum de Boston, cocuradora de la XXXIV Bienal de São Paolo y curadora del programa de performance, música, poesía y texto *Idiorhythmias*, en el Museo de Arte Contemporáneo de Barcelona (MACBA). Fue directora y curadora de la Galería del REDCAT de Los Ángeles de 2012 a 2018, y curadora jefe del Museo de Arte Carrillo Gil de Ciudad de México de 2007 a 2012. Es fundadora, en 2010, de LIGA-Espacio para arquitectura, una plataforma sin ánimo de lucro basada en la experimentación entre arquitectura, urbanismo y arte público en América Latina.

*haudenschild*Garage

Fundado en el 2003 por Eloisa Haudenschild, el *haudenschild*Garage busca proporcionar plataformas culturales a través de las cuales se alienta a los artistas internacionales y locales a experimentar y participar en diálogos abiertos. La misión es ofrecer un contexto facilitador para la opinión y la producción. El *haudenschild*Garage colabora directamente con los artistas a través de los programas Projects and Commissions, Garage Talks, Fuel4Talks y Artist Residencies.

Acknowledgments

Haudenschild Family, Migdalia, Pilar and Aziel Rubio, Chris Shea Family, Osvaldo Sánchez, Michael Krichman, Carmen Cuenca, Brittney Osbahr, Carolina Sánchez, Jim Lennox, Julien Salabelle and Rinaldo Sata. Special thanks to Meyenberg´s collaborators: Natalia Pérez Turner, Martin de Torcy, Martha Uc, and Félix Blume.

Artist´s acknowledgments

To Chris Shea:

Thank you dear friend, for having opened a path between the plants, where we could find the perfect place for sharing a common ground: our truest fears and an irrevocable curiosity for an inebriating aesthetic of nature. We thank you for teaching us to see between the petals and find the wonders below, in the spaces between the shade and the hidden places of the plants.

To Eloisa Haudenschild:

Thank you Eloisa for having the vision and the intuition, for always supporting and letting this path between the leaves to be created. You are the one who keeps this space from collapsing and disappearing among all possible gardens.

Agradecimientos

Familia Haudenschild, Migdalia, Pilar y Aziel Rubio, familia de Chris Shea, Osvaldo Sánchez, Michael Krichman, Carmen Cuenca, Brittney Osbahr, Carolina Sánchez, Jim Lennox, Julien Salabelle y Rinaldo Sata. Un especial agradecimiento a los colaboradores del artista en el proyecto: Natalia Pérez Turner, Martin de Torcy, Martha Uc, y Félix Blume.

Agradecimientos del artista

Para Chris Shea:

Gracias, querido amigo, por abrir este camino entre las plantas, donde podemos encontrar el lugar perfecto para compartir un mundo común: nuestros verdaderos miedos y una irrevocable curiosidad por una estética embriagadora de la naturaleza. Te agradecemos por enseñarnos a ver entre los pétalos y a encontrar las maravillas que hay debajo, en los espacios en sombra y escondidos de las plantas.

Para Eloisa Haudenschild:

Gracias, Eloisa, por tu visión, siempre apoyándonos y dejando un espacio para crear entre las hojas. Tú eres la que evita que este espacio colapse y desaparezca entre todos los jardines posibles.

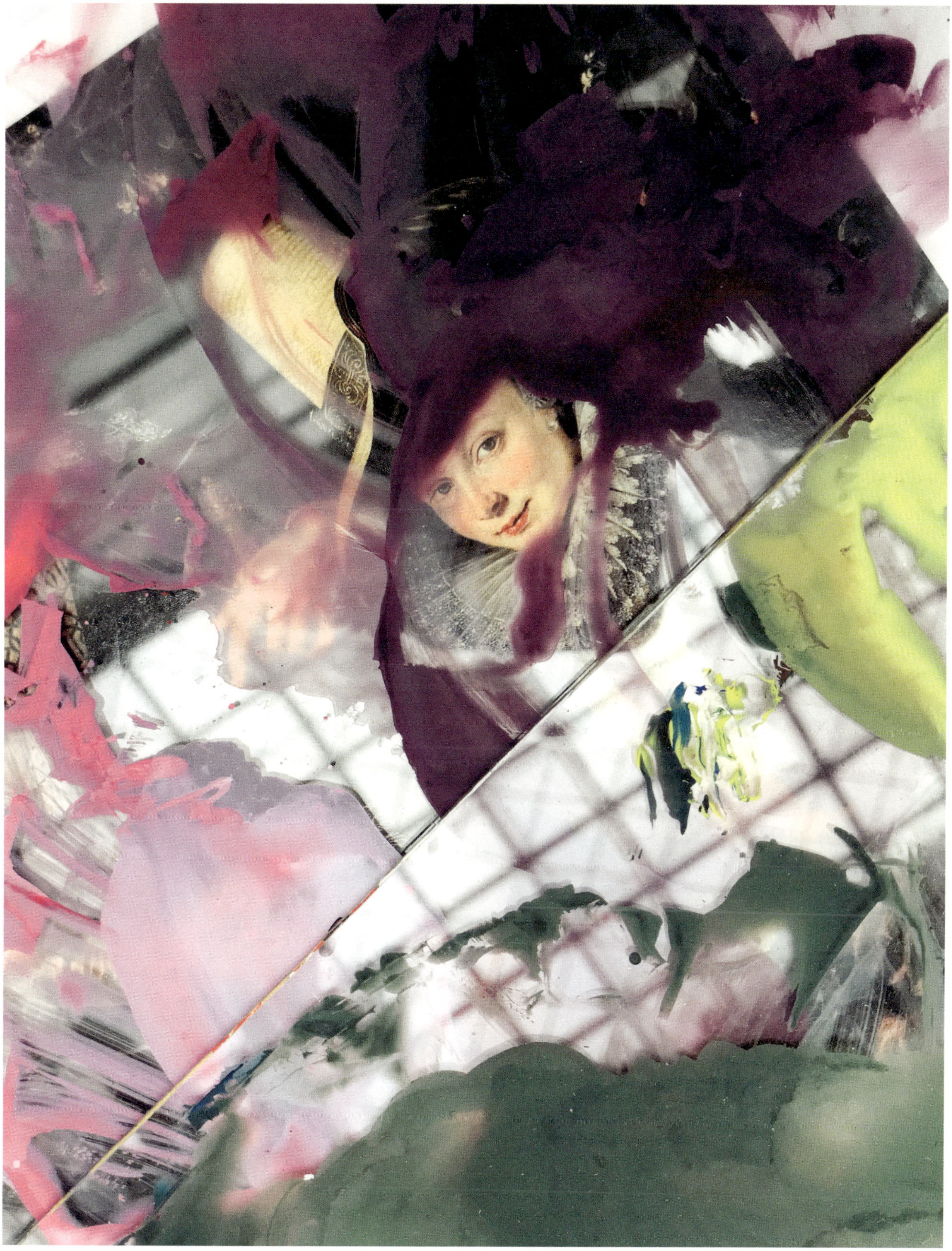

Even When Fall Is Here

This publication accompanies the project *Erick Meyenberg: Even When Fall Is Here*, September 5, 2016–August 11, 2018, at the *haudenschild*Garage, San Diego, California, commissioned by Eloisa Haudenschild.

Text: Ruth Estévez
Translator: Christopher Winks
Copy editors: Stacey Allan and Alicia Di Stasio
Designer: Jessica Fleischmann, still room
Printed and bound by Ofset Yapimevi, Istanbul, Turkey

ISBN: 978-1-7339579-1-5

Publisher's Cataloging-in-Publication Data
Names: Meyenberg, Erick, author. | Estévez, Ruth, author.
Title: Even when fall is here / Erick Meyenberg ; text by Ruth Estévez.
Description: Los Angeles, CA: Doppelhouse Press, 2019.
Identifiers: LCCN 2019949219 | ISBN 9781733957915
Subjects: LCSH Meyenberg, Erick. Works. | Shea, Chris, Works. | Gardens in art. | Gardens--Design. | Landscapes in art. | Landscape architecture--United States. | Artists' books--California. | Artistic collaboration--United States. | Multimedia (Art)--United States. | Bilingual books. | BISAC ART / Individual Artists / Artists' Books | ART / Subjects & Themes / Landscapes & Seascapes | GARDENING / Essays & Narratives
Classification: LCC ND1351.6. M49 2019 | DDC 758/.1/09794--dc23

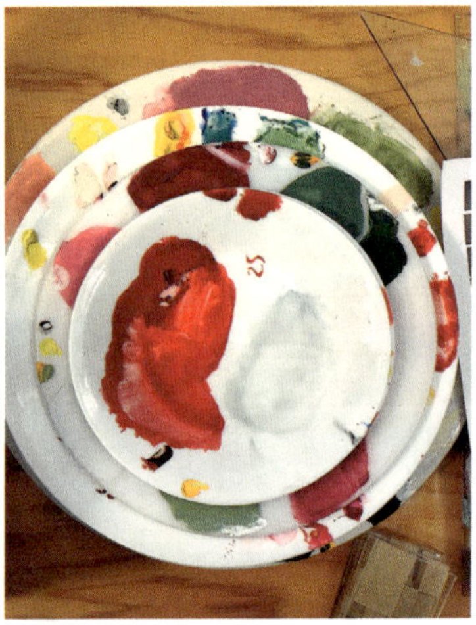

Pages 39-93:
Chris Shea's notebook with annotations by Erick Meyenberg (2015-2017)

Pages 122-129:
Color codes for the making of *Even When Fall Is Here* (2017)

Páginas 39-93:
Diario de Chris Shea con anotaciones de Erick Meyenberg (2015-2017)

Páginas 122-129:
Códigos de color realizados para *Even When Fall Is Here* (2017)

*haudenschild***Garage**
Doppel House Press